SOUL NUMBERS

SOUL
Numbers

DECIPHER THE MESSAGES FROM YOUR INNER SELF TO SUCCESSFULLY NAVIGATE LIFE

MICHELLE ARBEAU

Celebrity Numerologist, Author,
Inspirational Speaker, Radio/TV Host

OPEN ROAD

INTEGRATED MEDIA

NEW YORK

978-1-4976-6098-4

This edition published in 2014 by Open Road Integrated Media, Inc.
345 Hudson Street
New York, NY 10014
www.openroadmedia.com

CONTENTS

FOREWORD

11:11

Carrie White, Hollywood Hairstylist

Where to begin with "elevens and me?" I know where … my name Carrie White is an eleven.

It's curious, yet like an automatic robot my head seems to swivel like a magnet for my eyes to see 11:11 on my cell phone, a computer, or a clock, whether morning or evening. It's too consistent for over fifty years to be coincidence.

I had an affinity for Numerology when I first learned about it in the '60s. The evidence in my life confirms its truth. But that's a long story, so let me just begin with the conclusion of my memoir … which took me the last 22 years to write … which, by the way, is a number that takes two elevens to make.

Then it began like a tsunami. I say tsunami because it was unpredictable, unstoppable, and unbelievably huge by the time 11-11 rode itself out with my book.

Like I say, twenty-two years of writing, rewriting, stopping, starting over, cutting, editing, polishing until one day, I absolutely knew I was finished with my memoir. I pushed back from my desk. I had a tear in my eye, a smile on my face, and I knew beyond a doubt I was finally finished. My next thought after "I'm done" was "What's the date?" I looked at the calendar, and it was November 11th. Then I shouted out loud in my empty room, my quiet empty home, "Eleven eleven … it's eleven eleven!!"

I rushed to call my friend Bird who also has her eyes fixed at the stroke of 11:11 to her phone, computer or clocks because she would understand the magic of the date and this moment after knowing me all these twenty-two years working on my memoir. She screamed.

The very next day, I began the truly scary work of creating a request for my representation to the biggest agent in America, Lynn Nesbit. I had heard of her in the seventies, I knew one day I would write a book, and I wanted her to be my agent. This had not changed. I also knew approaching her in an email that it had to be perfectly worded to get her attention. When I finished, I realized it had taken me 11 days to compose because I was sending it on November 22nd, 2009 (2+9+11).

She replied immediately because our mutual beloved friend and client Michael Crichton had told her about my memoir, *Upper Cut, Highlights of My Hollywood Life* and me. She said, "I'd be happy to read your manuscript, send it to my assistant (electronically)."

On December 22[nd,] Lynn Nesbit called me at my salon. She told me she would like to try and sell my book and be my agent. My excitement was hard to contain. She said she would be off for the holidays, returning to her office the first week of January. At this time, she would draw up papers and send to me. I signed and sent them back to her on the day I received them: January 11th.

On February 22nd, she called with a publishing deal for Atria Books of Simon and Schuster. She told me they wanted to release *Upper Cut* for a summer read in July of 2012. I told her about all my elevens, and my book *had* to come out 2011. She humored me, "Carrie, we are in New York City, *you're in Hollywood.*"

Yet, the next day she called me back and said the publisher wanted my book out sooner and the new release date would be 2011 after all…

I finished more cutting and editing throughout the year of 2010. I decided it was time to meet everyone, and so I invited my agent, Lyn, my publisher, Judith Curr, Vice President and Senior Editor, Greer Hendricks, who worked with me cutting and polishing the book. Also joining us for lunch was the amazing Paul Olsewski, head of the PR division. It was the end of September, and I thought oh before Thanksgiving would be a good time, so I booked the second week of November. Not thinking of dates, I arrived on the ninth. The only time my people could meet with me was on Thursday, which was the one year anniversary of my book's completion: 11-11.

I told my new business friends at lunch all about my 11-11 stories. And to my surprise my publisher, Judith Curr, later emailed me an article about the coming year's celebration going on all over the world for 11-11-11. Numbers influence the world, why not the people in it? Do I need to say more?

I love Michele Arbeau, who found me on Facebook. It was through a series of connections and later she discovered I actually wrote about Numerology in my memoir. She did my numbers, and we were both jaw-dropped with all my 11s. She is a kindred spirit and earth angel. She was so accurate with me and told me things I didn't realize still influence me according to numbers and destiny arising from them.

She too has the 11:11 *thing* going on … it is quite unique, though the phenomena of seeing 11:11 everywhere seems to be catching on. Google 11:11 … it's a trip. People either have it and get it or say what are you talking about?

I rarely make a wish at 11:11 sightings … which is said to be what you do when you see it. I connect with that universe that called me to such an awareness. It's a specific internal clock that is bigger than making a wish. It's like information to me … a message from my higher power that I'm on time in my life and for me to remember where I came from. I do believe we are all here on a mission of service to connect and help people with others or themselves.

It's difficult to explain, it's a feeling, yet it's tangible. We can't capture rainbows in the palm of our hands, but we can see them clearer from a distance.

For me, 11:11 is a code calling card reminder of a power in operation, ancient and futuristic and most important: it is ONE plus ONE for ONE and all ONE.

Carrie White was born in Southern California. With a hairdressing career that has spanned more than forty-five years, she's styled everyone from Elvis Presley and Ann-Margret to Sandra Bullock and Brad Pitt. Her work has appeared in Vogue, Harper's Bazaar, InStyle, Allure, Vanity Fair, Ladies' Home Journal, Mademoiselle, *and* Glamour. *The mother of five, Carrie today owns and operates Carrie White Hair in Beverly Hills.*

Carrie White, author of Upper Cut, Highlights of my Hollywood Life, *published by Simon and Schuster/Atria Books, endorsed by Jackie Collins, Vidal Sassoon, and Publishers Weekly. Upper Cut debuted at #8 on the* Los Angeles Times *Best Seller list. Carrie is also a* Huffington Post Blog *contributor and keynote speaker for large and small audiences.* **www.TheCarrieWhite.com.**

CHAPTER 1: MY JOURNEY INTO THE WORLD OF NUMBERS

How Death, Dreams and a Joy Project Led Me to My Destiny

At the age of four, I died. It was only for a brief few minutes, but that experience changed the trajectory of my life forever.

I remember it like it was yesterday. I was playing with two other boys in a back bedroom down the hallway. We had been eating candies called Gobstoppers which were round, hard treats not suitable for a four year old to eat. I don't remember how the candy became lodged in my throat, but I do remember what followed.

I tried to tell the boys I couldn't breathe, but they thought I was joking and wouldn't let me out of the room. I kept gesturing in hopes they would understand and let me free. As my oxygen supply ran out, the room started to appear distorted as if I were in a big bubble. By the time the brothers figured out what was really happening and let me out, I barely made it into the hallway before I collapsed onto the floor in front of my mother. She heard the commotion and came to check on me.

My lips were blue, and I wasn't breathing. Suddenly, I appeared beside my body, and I watched my mother frantically trying to remove the candy from my throat with her finger. Strangely, I was completely calm while I watched. The degree of peace and safety I felt was something I had never experienced before. Standing beside me were two white light beings, and to this day I don't know who or what they were. Maybe angels, aliens, I'm not sure. All I know is that I felt safe, loved, and protected in their presence.

After I recovered from that experience, psychic phenomena began to constantly appear in my life. I had strange dreams, knew things about people that I shouldn't know, and, being such a young child, felt oddly different.

These experiences kept happening throughout my childhood, and when the teen years hit, it slowly began to intensify. I remember distinctly having a premonition at the age of nineteen that scared me to death. My mother and I were shopping in the grocery store when we happened to run into a friend of hers she hadn't seen in a while. I stood watching as they made small chit-chat when suddenly a wave of intense grief and sadness washed over me. I had yet to experience that degree of sadness in my life, and I felt as though a dam of tears was about to break. I told my mother I needed to go outside for some fresh air.

The next day my mother received a phone call informing her that her friend's long-time boyfriend had shot himself in the chest. She called me at home to tell me, but somehow I wasn't surprised.

These were the kinds of common occurrences that happened all the time in my life. I managed to push these experiences aside until my mid-twenties when my psychic reception took on a new twist.

At the age of twenty four, just after my first child was born, I started dreaming in numbers every single night. Psychic dreams were nothing new to me, but seeing numbers were a new element I had never experienced. The phenomena lasted for three months, and I documented every number message on a notepad that lay on my night table.

At the time, I had no idea what these number messages meant, but I had a strong intuitive sense that this was something momentous. In my quest to decipher the number codes, the first book I stumbled upon was Doreen Virtue's "Angel Numbers 101." I was blown away at what the numbers meant. Every single number message was an answer to the challenges and obstacles I was facing in my life at the time. There was no doubt that the numbers were guiding messages from beyond.

Ravenous for more answers, I began scouring the internet for information. Every search led me to numerological information, and the rest, as they say, is history. I fell in love with numbers and numerology. In hindsight, I realized that numbers were always my gift. I had a photographic memory for numbers and only had to see a phone number, address, or account number once to remember it.

After teaching myself the science of numerology in a matter of days (which I assimilated at an extremely rapid pace), I could literally "see" numbers and their meanings at a deeper level. It was unmistakably my gift, my path ... my purpose.

I had a few mentors in my life that were helping me get a handle on my psychic abilities, but I had no idea how I was going to share this new found gift of numbers with the world.

Through the assistance of these mentors, I began to use my psychic talents for others, but I was extremely shy about doing so. My fear of being judged and criticized was crippling, and I was always making excuses or rationalizing my intuitive abilities to clients. I began using numerology as my go-to tool in sessions with others, giving my numerical two-cents to back up my intuitive hits. Using the numerology as a crutch, it was a way for me to feel safe in using my intuitive gifts without the risk of being judged. In my mind, it was the numbers (and not me) giving the client the answers they were seeking, so the pressure was off.

I started off with the title of Intuitive Numerologist and began doing client sessions in a professional way. Fast-forward several years later, and I had built a steady practice, was writing my first book and had already been recognized by local media for my work. Things seemed like they were on the upward swing on the outside, but on the inside, something wasn't right. Bubbling just below the surface were big life changes.

The pivotal moment occurred when Brit Celeb Radio on LA Talk Radio invited me to be a guest on their show via phone to profile a "Pirates of the Caribbean" actor. I was thrilled about the opportunity but also nervous because it was my first "celebrity" session. I ended up making a friend that day that changed the course of my life. The actor's name was Treva Etienne, and he called me after the radio interview to personally thank me for the reading. We talked for some time, and really connected with each other. It was the start of a friendship I cherish to this day.

More synchronicity came in the form of an invite to a Hollywood party. I was invited to an AMA after party by Treva's publicist. This would be my first taste into the real world of celebrity and, coming from a small town, it was an eye-opening experience. I was Los Angeles bound and about to truly embrace my calling.

There's just something special about California. I never anticipated I would become smitten with it considering I don't watch much TV, and I'm not a follower of Hollywood at all. The glitz and glamour of Hollywood isn't my cup of tea, yet there's something that draws me there; I can't put my finger on it. It feels like home to me, and even after many trips under my belt, I always look forward to going back the moment I leave.

It only seemed fitting that I start my journey in Los Angeles. My soul-searching really began there. My British friend Treva, one of the most authentic people I know, pointed out that I wasn't living my truth. He could see through my people-pleasing ways and felt it was critical to explore my inner self if I was ever going to be truly happy. I already knew this, but to hear it from another really struck a chord in me. Being the people-pleaser, I let others take my power and put on a smiley face, even if I was shattered inside. I looked to others for the right answers instead of listening to my own intuitive inner voice. Living for and through others was killing me, inside and out.

After that conversation with my friend, I flew home the next morning. I barely remember the flights. I came back a changed woman. I experienced a profound shift with my inner self sometime between that conversation and my arrival home.

I knew I couldn't live a lie anymore. I stripped myself of all my titles, stopped taking clients and shelved the book I was writing. I was suddenly nothing and no one, but at least I wasn't living someone else's vision of me any longer. I felt naked and relieved, but I wasn't sure how to go about finding the real Michelle from here.

I admitted to myself that I wasn't genuinely happy in my life, and true joy and happiness were lacking in my day to day living. I had to start somewhere, so I began with a search on the internet for information on joy and happiness. The second pivotal piece of the puzzle revealed itself. I found the quote by John Templeton "… *To get joy, we must give it, and to keep joy, we must scatter it.*"

It was a total ah-ha moment. My mind was going a mile a minute. The Give Joy Now project was born in a matter of days, and it would become the second catalyst in my journey to becoming whole, happy, and living on purpose.

The Give Joy Now Project was a creation meant to help us find joy and happiness by giving it to others, as John Templeton's quote references. I had small, round stones called Joy Gems, business cards and a website created, got a sponsor for the Joy Jeep labeled up with the official logo, and had the vision of travelling the countryside spreading joy. In return, I hoped to find a little joy of my own.

Thankfully my husband and I were feeling the same way. We were both at a major crossroads in our lives, and drastic times call for drastic measures.

So there I sat, in a room nearly empty with a couple of packed boxes at my feet. I had sold my house, let go of most of my personal possessions, and was set to head out on the journey of my life. I wasn't sure where this journey was going to take me or even if it would be successful, but it didn't matter. I just knew I had to try to find the real me, or I'd regret it forever.

With two kids, a dog, a jeep and a trailer in tow, our little family headed across Canada handing out the small glass stones called Joy Gems to random strangers with the challenge to perform one random act of kindness for another, then passing the Gem on to the joy receiver to continue the joy-filled momentum. We had no timeline or schedule, and our destination was joy.

Nine days into the journey, we made it as far as Calgary, Alberta, where we ended up staying. We had a friend there. Feeling unsettled with no home base and nowhere to go, we decided to stop. That short stay ended up being almost two years and counting. It turned out to be the final pivotal puzzle piece in manifesting my calling.

Within weeks of being in Calgary, CTV (a major network in Canada) called me to be a guest on their morning show. I have no idea how they even knew I was in town.

This was my chance to reinvent myself. I had no title, no platform, and I was in a city that had no idea who I was yet. This was the moment to do what felt right to *me*.

It has been a snowball effect from the moment I arrived in Calgary. After rebranding myself as a Celebrity Numerologist, I've had a steady stream of media interviews, several new celebrity clients, two book deals, a successful online radio/TV network (Authentic You Media) and have my own downtown office space. A far cry from when I hit the reset button on my life just 2 short years ago.

It's amazing the difference when you live from the perspective of inner truth. I have nothing to hide, no excuses to make for being me, and I love who I am now. Ultimately, this is what I do for others in my work as a numerologist. I help them discover their truth through the numbers. We aren't meant to live someone else's version of the truth; we're meant to live our own.

It's been a long road to get to a place of true happiness and contentment with my life, and, most importantly, with me. I truly believe that in order to teach others something, you need to have gone through the experience yourself. This book is a culmination of my own journey to reveal and live my truth as well as my revelations with the world of numbers. Both are really one and the same. It is my desire and pleasure to be able to share the wisdom and knowledge I've gleaned from walking the path to truth and in the process, unlocking the secrets of life contained within the numbers. All that you need to reveal and live your truth right now is in your hands. As Pythagoras said, "Everything lies veiled in numbers."

CHAPTER 2:
THE HISTORY OF NUMBERS
The Creation and Enduring Nature of Numbers

Do you often notice that the same numbers repeatedly appear on your digital clock? Have you ever wondered why there just happens to be three fours in your telephone number? Has the same number shown up throughout your life so often you've adopted it as your lucky number? Are you one of the many who have diminished these repeating number patterns as sheer coincidence, or do you believe there is something more to these quirky occurrences?

For most of us, numbers are black and white symbols that we were taught to add, subtract, multiply and, divide. Numbers represent so much more than just mathematics. In fact, the numbers in your date of birth contain the image of your inner self and your life path—just as a seed contains an image of the plant it will grow into.

Through learning the science of numbers, you'll start to take note of the reoccurring patterns in your life and understand the meaning behind them. Imagine being able to predict the future and make informed choices instead of stumbling around in the dark, playing the guessing game. Numerology is not a mystical or magical art as many believe, it is pure science. Pythagoras believed the world was one big mathematical equation, and in my opinion, he was right!

Numbers, like all things, are energetic patterns. In metaphysics this is a fact, but science is now discovering what the metaphysical community has known for millennia—everything is made of energy. Quantum physicists say the atom is not matter, but frozen light particles that appear to be solid matter. Based on this new theory, by the scientific definition, what we think of as matter does not exist.

The late Noble Peace Prize winning physicist, David Bohm wrote in his book, "Wholeness and the Implicate Order"[1] that the universe is a sea of energy, and he saw the fundamental activity of nature as light. To Bohm, matter is not solid but rather condensed light. In other words, atoms, which are the basis of all matter, are comprised of frozen or slowed down light particles.

Pythagoras was a Greek mathematician and philosopher and was considered the father of the science of numbers. Pythagoras believed that everything in the universe could be represented by numbers. His belief was founded in the fact that all energy follows patterns (until interrupted), and because numbers are energetic patterns too, we can use the numbers as a window into the world of energy.

Most of the information and knowledge of Pythagoras about his work with numbers and his life was documented centuries after his death; therefore, the accuracy of his work and theories has been questioned by skeptics. One piece that was known to be true about Pythagoras is that he had a Mystery School where he taught his students that nothing could exist without numbers. He believed that mathematics formed the basis of all things in existence and that numbers were the essence of creation.

So astonishing were Pythagoras' findings that he swore his students to secrecy. The Pythagorean Society took an active part in politics which, unfortunately, led to the demise of the Mystery School and its following as the government did not approve of such a secret order[2]. The school and meeting places were burned along with much of the knowledge and information contained within them. The information that did survive was put together by followers and students of his work which is now the basis of modern Pythagorean Numerology.

This book is based on the work and teachings of Pythagoras as it is, in my opinion, the most scientific and accurate of all numerological systems.

Like electricity, all energy flows in predictable patterns. Energy is not erratic, but it flows to a rhythm and is in perfect harmony. Numbers are merely a way to visibly see these patterns and how they flow.

All numbers in existence are formed using the base numbers one to nine (also zero). Each digit from one to nine represents a specific and unique energetic pattern. In music, each note has a certain frequency or harmonic vibration. Just like musical notes, we all have our own vibration as does everything else in existence, including numbers.

By matching the vibration of a number to the vibration of anything in our world, we can gain understanding of its energetic pattern. Numbers act as a blue print or map that enables us to visually see and understand the energy within and around us.

Energy follows cycles because patterns repeat. History repeats itself. The human body is a very good example of this. All the cycles and processes in the human body follow predictable and consistent patterns. Our body and its processes are a mathematical work of art. Nature too follows patterns—like the seasons, moon cycles, and tides.

The processes in life are not by chance or coincidence, but a consequence of energetic patterns interacting with each other— cause and effect. If we join electricity with wood, it does not flow. If we join electricity with water, it flows. The world is not chaotic; it is full of rhythm, pattern, and harmony.

For example, the numbers in our date of birth give us an outline of our journey and how we travel that journey. It shows our own energetic pattern as well as the energetic patterns that have an influence on us during our life span. The numbers cannot show us the minute details of our lives because we cannot predict precisely how the energies will interact with each other. DNA gives us an outline of the human body, but it cannot show us whether we will die of cancer or develop Alzheimer's. It can give us an indication of our probability to develop such conditions, but it cannot predict with certainty. Like DNA, which gives us a map of our physical body, the numbers in our date of birth provide a blueprint of our inner self and our path.

When we are born, our DNA shows a perfect human being. Then, as time goes by, we make choices that affect this perfectness. We may choose to eat poorly, not exercise or any number of choices that negatively impacts the body. As with our bodies, we also have a choice when it comes to our journey in life. There are so many ways to arrive at the same destination. We have free will to choose to take the shortest path or the scenic route. We can choose the negative path filled with stress, loss, and sacrifice or we can make positive choices that allow the energy to flow effortlessly. Life is most certainly about the journey and not so much about the destination. Our choices have a big impact on how our energies will flow. Life is not supposed to be hard, because energy is meant to flow effortlessly and smoothly. If you find yourself hitting stumbling blocks and life seems difficult, it is a neon sign telling you to turn around and go the other way—like a magnet that repels or attracts.

Although Pythagoras is considered the father of numerology, numbers have existed for much longer than that. Bones and other artifacts have been discovered with marks cut into them that many believe are tally marks[3] used to measure things like time, lunar cycles, and quantifying objects. This rudimentary use of numbers and counting was built upon further by later civilizations into what we now know as mathematics.

The Mesopotamians are known more for their invention of writing, but they also played a part in the use of numbers in a mathematical way. Construction of irrigation systems, and later of temples, palaces, and other buildings required precise measurements. This resulted in the development of mathematics. The Mesopotamians used the sexagesimal numeral system (base 60) and all four mathematical operations (addition, subtraction, multiplication, and exponentiation), while the clay tablets from the Library of Ashurbanipal include quadratic and cubic equations, and fractions. Knowledge in geometry probably encompassed general rules for measuring areas and volumes. Mesopotamians also used π which was estimated as three.

The sexagesimal numeral system was also used for temporal measurement: year was divided into 12 months, month into 30 days, day into 2x12 hours, hour into 60 minutes, and minute into 60 seconds. The Mesopotamians also divided a circle into 360 degrees of 60 arc minutes. The priests observed and recorded the celestial phenomena from the temples, which also served as observatories. The priests composed various celestial maps and devices for calculating paths of celestial bodies, while the Babylonians knew to calculate the movements of the sun, moon, and planets, and to predict solar and lunar eclipses. The Babylonians used lunar calendar, which divided a year into 12 lunar months, and 11 days, while the New Year started in spring[4].

Numbers are also seen throughout the scriptures of the Bible. Many scholars believe there are deeper spiritual significances contained in the numbers that appear in the ancient scriptures. Still others believe the Bible is written as spiritual metaphors, and numbers may also be a part of these metaphoric messages. Even the religion of Kabbalah has a strong association with numbers and those who follow this belief system believe that every letter/word, number, even accent on the words contain deeper metaphysical meaning.

The Buddhist tradition uses prayer beads that act as counters for the number of times a mantra is spoken during periods of meditation. Some mantras are repeated as much as hundreds or thousands of cycles.

The Buddhist Prayer Beads typically contain 108 beads because it is believed we have 108 afflictions. We have six senses (sight, sound, smell, taste, touch, and consciousness) multiplied by three possible reactions (positive, negative, or indifference) forming 18 "feelings." Each feeling can be "attached to pleasure or detached from pleasure" creating 36 "passions," each of which can be manifested in the past, present, or future. Tallied together, these "afflictions" total 108.[5]

Aside from religion, the Chinese culture takes the meaning of numbers very seriously and pay top dollar to have an object with a particular number association. For example, the word "eight" sounds very similar to the Chinese word for "prosper," "wealth," or "fortune." In their culture, everything from telephone numbers to house addresses and names are selectively chosen for their numerical meaning. They firmly believe in a number being either auspicious or ill-fated.

Plato, the Greek philosopher and scholar, referred to numbers, the study of numbers as well as their meaning in this manner: "Numbers are the highest degree of knowledge. It is knowledge itself."

Superstitions, mythology, and fairytales contain number sequences. Have you ever wondered why we make three wishes or why there were seven dwarfs in the tale of Snow White? Do you have a favorite number or one that you avoid? The number thirteen became famously unlucky thanks to the superstitions of Friday the 13th and many hotels and airlines frequently eliminate the number thirteen to appease patrons.

There are numerous instances of numbers and counting used in various cultures and time-periods from the beginning of time onward, but there is a common thread amongst many of them. Numbers represent patterns (whether desired or not) and have a deeper meaning than just counting and mathematics.

Numbers contain a numerical language that if decoded reveals deeper meaning to help us successful navigate life. It could be argued that numbers were the first language dating as far back as the Stone Age. Carvings from the caveman era show stones marked with lines to count their bounties from hunting. Going deeper and further still, it may very well be the language of spirit. If you are one of many around the world who see repeating numbers and number sequences showing up regularly in your life, it could be that your soul has messages for you.

There's no denying the evidence. Could all of these cultures and belief systems be wrong? Is it just a coincidence that numbers are a common thread amongst all of them, or are numbers a coding system containing the secrets of life itself? Based on years of practicing the art of numerology, I have no doubt that numbers are the energetic patterns of creation.

This book is meant to be used as a tool in which to examine life through numbers as well as the patterns they represent. There are endless ways to examine the self and gain greater clarity of life, and there is no right or wrong way. Numbers are but one of those ways, but it's important to a method of self-analysis that resonates with you. Chances are, since you were drawn to and bought this book, numbers likely play a role in your life right already. Regardless of whether or not you become as passionate about numbers as I am, it is my desire that you finish this book with a greater understanding of yourself and the people around you.

I'm not one to accept anything on blind faith alone, so I wanted to start the book off with an ample serving of facts and figures to prime the pathway to your self-exploration. With an overview of the background and history of numbers from angles such as quantum physics, traditional science, religion, spirituality and mythology, you're ready to crack the code of self through the power of numbers.

CHAPTER 3: THE 9 ENERGETIC PATTERNS OF CREATION

The new theory in Quantum physics, string theory, states: "All objects in our universe are composed of vibrating filaments (strings) and membranes (branes) of energy."[6] This isn't technically a new theory, given the fact that the metaphysical community has believed this to be true for many centuries. However, it is a big step forward having the scientific community on board. Based on this theory, numbers are also energy and can act as a window into the unseen world of energy.

All numbers in existence are created using the base numbers one to nine. Zero is also included, but it is actually a symbol and not a number. It represents nothing and everything, the infinite. It is a neutral symbol representing the unmanifested (our goals and dreams which have not materialized into reality yet).

Any number, when added and reduced to a single digit, equals one of nine base numbers. Each number from one to nine has a specific meaning with specific traits and qualities because it represents a specific energetic pattern. A number, no matter where you see it, will have the same basic value or meaning. This is why numerology is highly accurate; it is a science, not a mystical art. It is simply matching a mathematical figure to something that has the same energetic frequency. There is no room for variance or error. It either matches or it doesn't.

These nine base numbers represent the nine base patterns of creation. All that you see in your world vibrates to an energetic frequency that can be matched with the energetic pattern of one of the numbers one to nine. You, the chair you're sitting on, the house you're in and the street you live on all carry an energetic pattern. What can knowing the vibrational pattern of a person, place or thing show you? It's like having a how-to manual for life. Numbers are the language of energy, and energy is at the basis of all there was, is, and will be.

For example, as a numerologist I work daily with the numbers in a date of birth. There are multiple digits in our birth dates, and so we have several different energetic patterns that influence us. Our main energetic pattern, the sum of our birth date, is our theme in this lifetime. It is the glasses through which we see the world. The individual numbers in our birth date are the traits and tools we can draw upon to assist us in achieving our purpose. If we use the example of a painter; the word "painter" is the theme, and the tools are the multitude of artistic talents, and painting supplies available to assist in fulfilling the role of painter.

Going further still, numbers can offer us a window into our path, lessons and goals we are meant to achieve, or experiences in this lifetime. All of this information can be uncovered simply by using the digits in our date of birth.

The day we were born holds the outline of our lives. Just like an acorn holds the image of the tree it will grow into. Numbers offer us a road map to follow, giving us choices along the way. Like a blueprint, numbers show us the main structure of the energy we have to work with, but we have a choice as to how we use the energy. There are infinite ways to the same destination but all, including numerology, lead to the same path.

Number messages are everywhere ... if you're willing to see them. They are the language of the universe, the code of creation, and wherever you see them, there is a message waiting for you to discover that could change your life. Whether it is a house address, license plate, phone number, employee code, or repeating digits on clocks or signs, there is a reason why that number has come into your awareness. Science has taught us that the world is not chaotic but a series of repeating patterns. The following nine base numerical patterns are the key to unlocking the mysteries of life.

THE THREE PLANES OF EXISTENCE

There are three planes of existence through which we experience life; the mind plane, the soul plane, and the physical plane. At any given time, we are operating from one or more of these three levels of existence. The mind plane represents the mental sphere, the soul plane represents the spiritual self, and the emotions and the physical plane represents the physical body and its actions. Each of the base numbers of one to nine resonate with a particular plane of existence. A base number is predominantly a mental energy, feeling energy, or a physical (doing) energy. For example, the lens through which you view the world is based upon which plane of existence your energetic pattern resonates in. Are you a thinker, a feeler, or a doer? Likewise, the numerical messages that appear in your world have a basis in one of the three planes of existence. Is the numerical message saying take action, heal an emotional wound, or tap into your creative power?

THE MIND PLANE NUMBERS 3, 6, 9

When we're thinking, dreaming, creating, or engaging in any other mental activity, we are working through the energetic patterns of the mind plane. Comprised of the number of imagination and memory (three), the creative expression and visionary number (six), and the idealistic, ambitious, responsible humanitarian (nine), this plane of existence is typically the brains behind the operation. The mind is a tool to create the experiences necessary for our soul's evolution.

THE SOUL PLANE NUMBERS 2, 5, 8

When we are emotionally charged, meditating, spiritually reflecting, or focused on any other heart based effort, we are working through the energetic patterns of the soul plane. Pulling together the three most emotionally and spiritually charged numbers, the soul plane is the home of that little inner voice that keeps the overzealous and sometimes overanalyzing mind plane in check and on track. If we choose to listen to its inner nudges. Joining forces on this plane is the sensitive, intuitive, and cooperative number (two), the heart-centered emotional based freedom of expression energy (five) and the wise, independent, assertive soulful leader (eight).

THE PHYSICAL PLANE NUMBERS 1, 4, 7

When we are painting a house, running a marathon, driving our car, or actively involved in any other physical based action, we are working through the energetic patterns of the physical plane. Ideas born in the mind plane then ignited with passion by the soul plane are then brought to fruition through the physical plane. Our body becomes the vehicle through which we live our life experiences. Taking action, in the physical sense, regarding our goals and dreams is an important part in creating the life we desire. This is the plane of existence where we make things happen and bring our dreams to life. The best and most effective way to learn is through personal experience. The expression "live and learn" is fitting here. This plane combines the pioneering trailblazer verbal self-expression number (one) with the practical, solid foundation-building energy (four) and the teaching/learning truth-seeker that craves learning through hands-on doing (seven).

THE BASE NUMBERS 1-9

The base numbers are like the primary colors, from which every other color is based in. Everything that makes up the physical plane is comprised of the vibrational essence of one or more of the numbers one to nine. There are no exceptions or gray areas. Each of these nine numbers has its own unique vibrational pattern and distinct positive/negative attributes. These nine numbers form the basis of what Pythagoras called the "science of numbers," and what we now call Numerology today.

The keywords that follow each definition give a summary of the traits and characteristics of each number meaning. Wherever you see a particular number, it will carry some or all of the keywords associated with it, depending on where you see it and how the energy is used. For example, a few of the traits of the number one are ambitious and aggressive. When analyzing an address vibration, the building isn't necessarily going to be ambitious or aggressive, but it may ignite these qualities in the homeowners.

THE BASE NUMBER MEANINGS
(ONE TO NINE AND ZERO)

1 One is the first physical plane number. It governs our communications skills and verbal self-expression through the ego. One is the only complete number, representing our divine expression through the physical. As the number most linked to ego, it is a driven and active energy, seeking achievement and success. **Keywords: verbal self-expression, initiate, action, ambitious, determined, pioneering, aggressive.**

2 Two is the first soul plane number. It represents our dualistic nature as spiritual beings in a physical body. The two represents our need to find balance between these two opposing sides of ourselves. Two is the number of intuition, sensitivity and cooperation. **Keywords: contrast, balance, cooperation, sensitive, intuitive, supportive, co-dependent.**

3 Three is the first mind plane number. As the imaginative yet rational and analytical number, it represents left-brain activity. Three is the number of imagination and memory and is particularly linked to the numbers one and two. Three's expression is directly tied to the intuitive and sensitive energy of the two and the verbal expression of the one. Three is symbolic of the mind (three), body (one), and soul (two) connection. **Keywords: analytical, intelligent, humorous, social, sensitive, observant, critical.**

4 Four is the middle physical plane number. It represents stability, steady progress, practicality, and organization. It is the anchor of the physical plane and is represented by the solid and stable construction of the square with its four equal sides. It is the most primitive of numbers. **Keywords: endurance, progress, foundation, practical, organization, solid, stable, materialistic.**

5 Five is the middle soul plane number and is also the central number on the birth chart. Five symbolizes the heart/emotions and as the center number, links the energies of all the other numbers. It is the heart and soul of the birth chart. Five must have freedom to express itself as by nature, it is an erratic, free-flowing energy pattern. The five energy lends us the ability to see the world through the eyes of the soul. **Keyword: loving, sensitive, irregular, artistic, freedom-seeking, passionate, uncertain.**

6 Six is the middle Mind Plane number. It links both the three (left-brain) and the nine (right-brain). It is the number of extremes with both a strong positive and negative side. Six has an enormous amount of creative potential as the number of creativity. When not positively creating, it can slip into the opposite (and negative) side of creativity ... destruction. In the negative, six is dominated by worry, anxiety and other negative thought patterns. In the positive, six can act as the "balancer" of the mind plane with its responsible, nurturing, and peace-maker qualities. **Keywords: creative, responsible, nurturing, home-loving, peace-maker, doting, worry-wart, people-pleaser, hostess, gossipy.**

7 Seven is the last and most active physical plane number. As the teaching/learning number, it is high "doing" energy. Seven learns through personal experience (often through hindsight), preferring to leap first and think later. Sacrifice and loss tend to be the rule of thumb for the seven energy. Such learning sets the stage for the accumulation of a tremendous amount of knowledge and wisdom in a short amount of time, making seven the self-made wise sage. **Keywords: wise, contemplative, achiever, determined, stubborn, active.**

8 Eight is the last and most active soul plane number. It represents wisdom and independence. Eight is confident, assertive, naturally wise and very much a leadership energy. Yet, at the same time, eight is loving and tender. These conflicting aspects of the eight energy create its main lesson—to learn to recognize that openly expressing love and appreciation will not subtract from independence, but add to it. **Keywords: independent, wise leader, loving, assertive, confident, dynamic, detached, selfish.**

9 Nine is the last and most active mind plane number. Although nine represents the right brain, it also combines the attributes of the other two mind plane numbers, three and six. Ambition (three), responsibility (six) and idealism (nine) make up the whole essence of the nine energy. Despite the idealistic and driven nature of the nine, it is a seeker of peace and justice and is considered the humanitarian number. **Keywords: humanitarian, ambitious, responsible, justice-seeking, idealistic, unselfish, driven, opinionated, judgmental.**

0 Zero is not a number but a symbol of the infinite. It symbolizes nothing and everything—energy not yet manifested into the physical. Zero represents our spiritual potential. Those with one or more zeros in their date of birth have an inherent spiritual awareness, waiting to be brought to full fruition. When a zero shows up in a numerical message, it highlights the importance or urgency of the message. The more zeros, the more important the message is.

MASTER NUMBERS

The Master Numbers are the higher vibrating energetic versions of several of the base numbers (1, 2, 4, 6). They represent the number's more spiritual form. In certain instances, such as when analyzing the full sum of our birth date (main essence) or calculating our name's energy, it is beneficial to leave the sum unreduced to a single digit as it gives a more accurate view of the energetic pattern. The exceptions are if the sum adds to 10, 11, 22 or 33. They are considered the spiritually-based guiding energies of Earth Guide (10), Spiritual Guide (11), Master Builder (22) and Master Teacher (33). It is thought that they carry a greater responsibility to mankind in the sense that their energy is meant to be utilized in a broader sense and to have global reach.

With a firm handle on the base energies that make up the world we know, we're ready to explore which of these base patterns our own lives have been built with. We are all one of the base numbers from one to nine, and the next chapter will take us on the journey to discovering what our main essence or energetic pattern is all about. Are you an analytical and imaginative three, an intuitive and sensitive two, or an action-seeking, hindsight learning seven? Knowing which main energetic pattern is yours can reveal the theme of life or the glasses through which the world is viewed.

CHAPTER 4: DISCOVER YOUR MAIN ENERGETIC PATTERN

Knowing Your Energetic Pattern Is the Key
to Unlock the Door to Self-Awareness

LIFE THEME NUMBER

Many numerology books call the sum of a date of birth the Life Path number, but this title is misleading. The sum of our date of birth does not show us the direction we will take in life. Rather, it is the overtone or theme of our life. Our Life Theme Number is a culmination of all the numbers/energies in our date of birth, combining to form the "theme" energy of our lives. Each individual number in our date of birth is a part of the whole, the whole being the sum of our birth date. The individual numbers in our date of birth are the puzzle pieces, that when joined together, form a complete and whole picture of our energetic essence.

The Life Theme Numbers section elaborates further upon the base number meanings. Keep in mind, a number is a number, no matter what form. However, the base number energies are like shell energies, the basic form of each vibrational pattern. They show us what the base numbers become when they are animated within a living form. For example, a rock may have the same energetic pattern as the base number nine, but it is not capable of displaying the humanitarian qualities of the nine energy. This can only occur when the soul is present.

The Life Theme Numbers section details what it is like to literally live and breathe the nine base energetic patterns that make up our world. You are one (or more) of these nine patterns, this you cannot change, but it is up to you how you choose to use your energy. Knowledge is power so empower yourself!

LIFE THEME NUMBERS
Calculating your Life Theme Number:
The individual numbers in our date of birth are like the secret code to unlock the door to our essence. Although our birth date digits also have influence on us, the Life Theme Number represents our essence, the foundation from which we build our lives. To calculate your Life Theme Number, add each individual number in your date of birth.

Using the birth date of December 8, 1978:

(MM/DD/YYYY)

1+2+8+1+9+7+8 = 36

If the total is a double digit, reduce again to one of the nine base numbers. (**NOTE: if double digit is ten, eleven or twenty-two, do not reduce further.)

3+6=9

The Life Theme Number for this date of birth is nine. If a birth date adds to a double digit number prior to reducing to a single digit, it can create a new shade of that main number. The example above adds to thirty-six prior to reducing to nine. Although the main energetic pattern remains a nine, this pattern is also working the numbers three and six in addition to the nine. The numbers present before reducing to a single digit represent the other qualities that make up the whole essence. These numbers are not as powerful or significant as the sum of the birth date reduced to a single digit, but they can show us the more subtle energies at work within us. They are usually our best hidden qualities, but are often unrealized and can represent our greatest challenge areas. The nine represents this birth date's main energetic overtone, but the three and the six energies create a new shade of the nine energy. There are many different shades of a color yet all originate from the same base color.

At the end of each Life Theme Number description is a chart detailing the other numbers that may be working with that particular energy.

3, 6, 9 — THE MIND PLANE NUMBERS

Those working a mental theme in this lifetime have one of the harder incarnations in terms of getting the job done in the physical sense, because they spend a great deal of time in their head and not taking physical action. The mind is ego's playground, and this is where we can often become snagged along the way. As humans, our mind is both our greatest tool and our biggest obstacle. Those who predominantly live through the mind are constantly facing the battle of ego versus soul. At times, they face excessive fears, worry, anxiety, depression, and a host of other negative mental activities that hinder accomplishment of goals. They can be exceptionally mentally keen, and there is no shortage of inspired ideas. When it comes to bringing those ideas to a reality, the negative mental aspects can easily take hold. The mental-based person often has a hard time moving from the mind and implementing their plans. Through utilizing the emotional passion of the soul plane, they then take action through the energy of the physical plane. In order to bring an idea to life, we not only have to think it, we need to feel it, and, most importantly, you need to *do* it.

LIFE THEME NUMBER 3 — "THE INTELLECTUAL SOCIALITE"

The number three is considered the gateway number to the mind plane. It is the number of the imagination and memory and is the most active number on the mind plane. With a mind like a computer, the suave three can charm the pants off anyone. Coming up with a perfectly executed and brilliant response to any social situation is mere child's play. However, three has no patience for stupidity and automatically expects everyone to be as smart as them. When someone doesn't meet a three on the same mental wavelength, they can suddenly shift gears from cool to callous, turning their positive mental energy into negative criticism.

The Life Theme Number 3 energy is fun, social, sunny, witty, intelligent, clever, imaginative, playful, analytical, and sometimes critical.

Bright Side of 3 (living through spirit)

Incredibly bright with minds that could dance circles around many, the three is master of the mind. With a memory like a calculator and an imagination bordering on insanity, they are the keeners of society. Threes are the socialites, always knowing what to say, when to say it, and how to say it. There are two key ingredients to the social success of the three: mental keenness and heightened emotions. When we put our feelers out in social situations, looking for the right way to respond, we use both our intellect and our intuition. As the number of imagination and memory, threes are quick to sum up a situation and come up with a winning response by not only using their lightning-fast minds but their heightened intuitive senses.

Three is a strong mental number, but it is also closely linked to the two, which is the first soul plane number representing the qualities of intuition and sensitivity. Three sits just above the two on the birth chart, therefore takes on many of its qualities. Threes have rather large emotional bodies and are often considered "empaths" because they can pick up psychic information from others through their emotions. Three is also strongly linked to the one, which sits below the two on the birth chart. One is the number of verbal self-expression and communication, which threes excel at. The expressive nature of the three utilizes the qualities of all the numbers three, two and one.

Dark Side of 3 (living through ego)

Three is the least serious and most fun of the mental energies, although criticalness of those who aren't as intellectually advanced is one of the less appealing sides of the three. They expect everyone else to be as sharp as they are, and they have little patience for stupidity. This air of mental superiority can paint the three as a bit of a snob at times. Ironically, the three is quite critical of others, and yet one of their greatest weaknesses is receiving criticism. A three can dish it out, but they can't take it. They are simply crushed by any amount of criticism however well intentioned. Their huge and very sensitive emotional bodies can't take the sting of such remarks. The three holds onto critical remarks from others and often collect it as mental and emotional baggage. They aren't ones to let it slide off their back or work through it easily. They even create baggage from being highly critical of themselves.

This collection of negative "baggage" accentuates the threes' biggest weakness of all— doubt. The three swims in a sea of self-doubt, swinging from feeling like they can do anything to a "what was I thinking" mindset. Heightened emotions combined with an overly imaginative mind, creates an atmosphere for the highs and lows, similar to a bipolar personality. They over-think and over-feel things to the point of beating a dead horse. Turning the mind off is hard for a three because that is their starting point, their home-base.

GREATEST CHALLENGE

The greatest challenge of the three is to step down from the mind plane and overcome their self-doubt. To do this, they need to practice spontaneous action with less thought involved. Stepping down from their comfort zone of the mental sphere and engaging in physical action is a huge hurdle for the three who would rather imagine doing something than actually do it. The fear of failure and criticism that goes along with the self-doubt holds them back. Unless they have a significant portion of their birth date numbers in the physical plane ("doing" plane), they struggle to bring their inspired ideas to a reality.

Soul to Soul Connections

The critical side of the three is most evident in their close relationships, particularly intimate ones. For a three, being overly critical of their mate is often the main reason for divorce. Their doubtful nature also causes them to question whether they have made the right choices in love, which can doom their relationships before it has a chance to blossom fully.

On the flip side, a three's sensitive emotional body gives them the ability to love deeply and passionately. Sometimes, depending upon how many emotional wounds they have acquired, their first response can be to guard their emotions, preferring to stay in the mental realm, where they feel safe. Once trust and respect for each other has been firmly established, the three can be a loyal and loving life partner. As parents, the three's love for their children can border on smothering.

Body Talk

The three's strong tie to the sensitive two energy sitting below it on the birth chart paves the way for collecting and holding onto an enormous amount of emotional debris. This includes not just their own but everyone around them. Threes also tend to be grudge-holders, storing those chips away deep within the body. This debris accumulates over time and manifests as unexplained aches and pains. Many threes suffer from unexplained pains and arthritic symptoms from the buildup of mental and emotional baggage. Each time the three suffers emotionally, their first response is to internalize it rather than deal with it outwardly. This is partly due to their mental nature but also because they are so sensitive to any form of emotional hurt, especially criticism. Emotional pain is literally crippling to them.

Path of Service
Threes are the writers, motivational speakers, inventors, scientists, and natural counselors. They excel in areas where a sharp mind is needed, but they are happiest when their path also involves emotionally uplifting others. Their work needs to have a good cause behind it. Threes are all about mental and emotional expression.

LIFE THEME NUMBER 6 — "THE CREATIVE GENIUS"

Six, as the middle Mind Plane Number and number of creation/creativity, is a deceivingly clever energy. On the surface, the six energy is the responsible "balancer." It provides some much needed balance to the imaginative three and the idealistic nine energies. Sixes are often the peace-makers and the more practical of the mental energies. However, beneath the surface, six energy is turbulent and has both a strong positive and negative side. It is often referred to as the number of extremes and for good reason. Six has an enormous amount of creative power, but when this creative juice is not used for positive creation, it slips into the opposite of creation - destruction.

As it is the middle number on the mind plane, this destructive energy is created through mental thoughts. Worry, anxiety, depression, fear, and a multitude of other self-destructive thought pattern makes up the six energy when living in the negative. The simplest and only remedy for the six is to create — period. Six must keep the creative energy flowing to stay out of the negative. Even small acts qualify, but, for the six energy to be happy and achieve long-term success, they must take their creative energy out into the world at large. Due to being home loving and nurturing, the six often gravitates toward creating only within the home and family. However, this soon leads them to negativity as their creative energy becomes pent up from underuse. They have such an abundance of creative energy that the only solution is to keep it flowing at a rate that will not allow it to become dammed up. Essentially, their creative energy is meant to be shared with the world not just within their own.

The Life Theme Number 6 energy is creative, loving, nurturing, unselfish, responsible, moral, moody, anxious, depressive and obsessive.

Bright Side of 6 (living through spirit)
Home-loving, nurturing and doting, the six is full of nesting energy as the "mother" of creative energy. Sixes are the peace-makers and problem-solvers in the family, the balancers. Responsible and reasonable they are always eager to please. People with six as their main essence (Life Theme Number) are deeply loving and selfless humanitarians. They are visionaries with their creative drive tuned toward the growth of all. So full of creative power, the six literally has the potential to achieve anything they set their mind to. The trick is for them to stay out of the negative mental vortex by keeping their creative juices flowing at a steady pace.

Creative energy is perfect and complete; therefore, the six has a perfectionist quality. This trait helps to propel them toward great success because they settle for nothing but their very best. However, perfectionism, with its judgmental and critical qualities in the negative, can be destructive to both the six and those around them.

Dark Side of 6 (living through ego)
The extreme need to be people-pleasers causes the six to frequently fall victim to the door-mat syndrome—used and abused. When their

creative energy is stalled, they begin feeling insecure from the loss of power and seek strength from others opinions of them. It becomes a "high" for the six to feel needed and appreciated, but what they are really lacking is their own creative power from within. When they are disconnected from this power, ego takes hold and insecurity and doubt creep in.

As the martyr energy, six can become so wrapped up in their responsibilities that it consumes every aspect of their lives. They can become so overwhelmed with worry and anxiety that it borders on delusional thinking. The six loves to play the "what-if" game, thinking of mental scenarios that probably will never occur in real life, even if they appear plausible in their head. This, of course, is their creative genius at work but in all the wrong ways. Over time, if the six remains in the negative long-term, these mental thoughts become reality in the form of excessive drama in their lives. The statement, "what we think about, we bring about" is so true in the life of a negative six.

Those close to the negative six are treated to a variety of nasty behaviors such as gossip, possessiveness, fault-finding, and whiny nagging, which only adds to the drama. This is the ego's way of creating and this kind of pattern can cause the six to spiral into defeatism and despair, a vicious cycle that is hard to break. Real creativity does not come from ego, and the six needs to constantly remind themselves of this.

GREATEST CHALLENGE

The biggest obstacle of the six is to achieve balance by seeking power within instead of looking to others opinions of them to feel good about themselves. Their perfectionism is meant to help manifest their creative visions and not to be used to belittle themselves or find fault with others. Constant positive creation is the cure-all for less than perfect side of the six.

Soul to Soul Connections

Deeply loving and always seeking to please, the six can be a terrific spouse, mother, and friend. Constantly concerned about the well-being of others, they easily forget their own needs. They are always a shoulder to lean on with their nurturing energy. This can be a win-win situation in the beginning of a relationship as the six feels fulfilled in being able to please others. In the long run, resentment and unfulfillment can set in. The greatest challenge of the six lies within the. They must learn to find that balance between give and take, which is the essence of a great relationship. It feels great to give selflessly, but our energy cannot remain balanced if we allow all of it to flow away from us because we are then left feeling empty.

Body Talk

The constant pull toward negative thought patterns puts the six at risk of stress related digestive disorders. They are not able to fully assimilate their abundance of both positive and negative ideas, and so they accumulate in the stomach and bowel regions causing conditions such as heartburn, ulcers, and a variety of bowel conditions. Women are especially prone to reproductive blockages, as the womb represents the seat of creativity. When creativity is stalled and stagnant long-term, the physical manifestation of this blocked energy often becomes apparent in the reproductive organs. Conditions such as fibroids, endometriosis, ovarian cysts, and infertility can result from blocked creative energy manifested by chronic negative thought patterns.

The tendency to accumulate excess emotional and mental baggage is a life-long struggle for the mind-dominant six. A constant and conscious effort to dwell in only positive thoughts is a must. There are physical remedies that can help to loosen the years of energetic sludge clogging the "pipes" and preventing positive energy from flowing. Blocking unwanted energy from external sources is very helpful in preventing further accumulation of emotional and mental energy. To prevent picking up energy from people, places, or things, simply imagine a bubble of white light surrounding you. This white light bubble will act as a shield to prevent further energy from penetrating and polluting the energetic bodies. Sea salt or Epsom salt baths are also a great way to rid the energetic bodies of "debris."

Path of Service
A field in which the creative power of the six is put to good (and constant) use is of the utmost importance if the six is to find life-long success. Creating for the sole purpose of money and power is not in alignment with the humanitarian style of the six. To feel fulfilled, the six must have an ethical and humanitarian purpose behind their work. Combining their active minds with their loving nature makes them top-notch performers—expressive and dramatic. Whether they grow up to be artists, writers, inventors, or designers, the six must continually create to remain balanced and content.

LIFE THEME NUMBER 9 — "THE AMBITIOUS AND IDEALISTIC HUMANITARIAN"

Nines are big thinkers and dreamers with a heart of solid gold. A nine wouldn't hesitate to give their last buck or the shirt off their back to a complete stranger. They're driven, determined, and opinionated justice-seekers, but underneath all these seemingly egotistical qualities is a deep love of people.

In addition to its own qualities, the nine contains the qualities of the other two mind plane numbers. Nine's main qualities are ambition (3), responsibility (6), and idealism (9). These three qualities make the nine an unstoppable force. Nine is a powerhouse energy that has limitless potential to achieve, as seen during the last century where nine was in every birth date. The nine forms the head of the Arrow of Great Expression (created by the joining forces of 7, 8 and 9 on the Birth Chart) and has been responsible for the incredible amount of progress achieved during the last one hundred years. The nine also forms the head of the Arrow of Determined Effort (created by the joining forces of 1, 5, and 9 on the birth chart, more on Arrows in chapter six).

The Life Theme Number 9 energy is ambitious, responsible, idealistic, justice-seeking, dreamer, honest/trustworthy, unselfish, opinionated, black and white thinker, impractical, serious, judgmental and hypocritical.

Bright Side of 9 (living through spirit)

In the positive, the nine Life Theme Number is the out-of-the-box big dreamer who is never short on ideas and viewpoints. As the "humanitarian," it is gentle leadership energy (for the people) and many great leaders of the past such as Gandhi and Mother Teresa have carried this main energetic frequency.

When centered in their power, people who are affected by the nine have the brain of a computer, the drive of a workhorse, and the nurturer nature of a mother bear. It is a combination that is unstoppable in terms of success and achievement in life. The nine is happiest when focused on anything that is bettering humanity or righting the wrongs of the world. Although not great in business, since they're big dreamers who often miss the finer details to give a project liftoff, they make a fine addition to any team because they are visionaries in their own right. The motto of the nine: "Go big or go home."

Dark Side of 9 (living through ego)

The key to success for the nine is not to allow their energy to get caught up in their tendency for black and white or right and wrong thinking. The nine is passionate about what they believe in, and their own firm beliefs can box them in and limit their creative power.

Judgmental and critical of both themselves and others, they can rival a six for the title of "Negative Nelly." Stuck in their strong ideals, they become rigid and set in their ways. Anyone who knows a nine understands that sometimes there's no changing their mind. After all, the nine does form the head of the Arrow of Determined Effort (Arrows are defined in chapter six) with its stubborn and pigheaded energy. It can become a slippery negative slope for the nine, and it is imperative, depending on the particular nine, to be surrounded by positive people, places, and things to broaden the horizons again. Carrying both the qualities of the three and six, it's no wonder the nine can also easily succumb to negative mind chatter that cripples their visionary momentum.

GREATEST CHALLENGE

The greatest challenge for the nine is to remain selfless in their humanitarian and idealistic efforts. Although their selfless desire makes them true givers, when in the negative they often get caught up in a "you owe me" outlook. Their justice-seeking energy wants the scales to always remain balanced. When a nine gives too much while receiving very little, over time the injustice can eat away at them causing a "chip on the shoulder" kind of energy to form. They then become cynical and jaded rather than the big dreamer they were meant to be. Remembering that their underlying drive is to be of service to others, regardless of whether they receive or not, will keep the nine from feeling like life has been cruel and unfair to them.

Soul to Soul Connections

A nine makes for some of the best parents, spouses, and friends in the world. If you're lucky enough to have one in your life, never take them for granted. As parents, they hold such immense pure love for their children, and this is where their selflessness shines through. The word love adds to nine, making the Life Theme Number nine the embodiment of unconditional love. As spouses, they are the rock of the relationship, and as a friend they've got your back to the very end. On the job, a nine is often the idea generator.

Relationships can be a challenge for a nine when they are with someone who is a taker. Since they are endless givers, they will eventually feel used and abused in a relationship that does not show adequate appreciation. At the end of the day, to show a nine how much you appreciate them is all that is required to replenish their endless pot of giving.

Body Talk

Many nines are over-analyzers with their big thinking energy. As the most active mind plane number, their brain is like a mouse wheel, forever spinning and churning out ideas. Stress and anxiety can get the better of them, and one of the most common ailments of a nine is headaches. The tremendous amount of mental energy creates "pressure" in the head. Physical exercise is a must to keep the nine grounded and allow for releasing of some of that pent up mental energy. Based on my own experience with my clients, those whose children have been labeled as having ADHD or ADD, frequently present with multiple nines in their date of birth. It is an interesting pattern that seems to be emerging and one that I will be following closely for further analysis.

Like the six, a nine can also suffer from digestive upsets such as heartburn or bowel trouble as they have even more active mind plane energy. However, unlike a six, who can remedy this through creative endeavors, a nine needs physical exertion or physical "pressure" to relieve the mental boiling pot. Since they are so black and white with their thinking, it is harder for them to shift mental gears. Anything that disengages the mind and engages the physical senses will go a long way in balancing the over-thinking nine.

Path of Service

Being an uneven number, a nine isn't usually great with the day to day operations in business. The finer details aren't their thing at all, and their energy is best utilized in planning or visionary efforts. Although big dreamers and visionaries, their ideas aren't always the most practical. Careers where their inspirational and outside the box thinking is appreciated are a perfect fit, as well as positions that are about creating justice or acting as a humanitarian in some form. Teacher, lawyer, doctor, activist, detective, counselor, and social worker are all suitable and fulfilling roles for a nine.

2, 5, 8 — THE SOUL PLANE NUMBERS

Those working a soul or emotional based theme in this lifetime usually have the realm of relationships as their battlefield where the majority of their life lessons dwell. They are deeply feeling, sensitive, and caring people who sadly often develop walls and armor at an early age to block and protect their sensitive souls.

On a positive note, the soul plane numbers are home to the intuitive self, which is an essential part of successfully navigating life. We rely on the energy of the feeling numbers in social situations to intuitively respond and appropriately react. For example, those who lack all three of the soul plane numbers come across as socially handicapped and are frequently misunderstood when trying to interact with others. Our emotional or soulful self is essential in interacting with other souls. When we are out of touch with that side of ourselves we are most certainly struggling in some way, shape, or form. Of the three realms of existence (mind, soul, physical), the soul plane is the most essential to our wellbeing.

Life Theme Number 2 — "Supportive Guide"

They say behind every great leader is a two. Not a fan of the spotlight, a two works best behind the scenes offering support, intuitive guidance, and sensitive as well as gentle encouragement. Of all the Life Theme Numbers, the two is the most uncommon. Only birth dates that total twenty can create this energetic pattern. Although the eleven reduces to two (1+1=2), the only true two first adds to twenty, combining the sensitive and intuitive two with the zero, which is the symbol of the infinite or spiritual awareness. As the number that most resonates with the soul and being the most sensitive soul plane number, the two is a peacekeeper who is all about balance, only

43

wanting life to be harmonious and cooperative.

The Life Theme Number 2 energy is contrast, balance, cooperation, sensitive, intuitive, supportive, co-dependent, uncertain, submissive and passive.

Bright Side of 2 (living through spirit)

This Life Theme Number is the least motivated by ego or driven for personal gain, and therefore is much more malleable and adaptable than most. Lacking the physical and mental drive and determination of numbers like the three, six and nine, this soul based number works from intuition. Money, materialism, and achievement for the self are not top priorities. Being the most emotionally and spiritually sensitive of all numbers, if a two is forced to live through any other plane than the spiritual, they become frustrated and emotionally irritated. Too much analyzing or thinking (mind plane) or being pushed toward aggressive drive and achievement (physical plane) and it can throw the two completely off balance. As with any Life Theme Number, it is important to develop the missing qualities to become more whole and balanced, but the two should keep the soul plane as their home base. They are mediators, not initiators and are not demanding or forceful by nature. Their intuitive skill is the heart of who there are and should remain the focal point in their lives. Through their strong intuitive skill, they are able to see both sides of a situation clearly, which makes them phenomenal visionaries and guides. The two leads through gentle nudging rather than taking charge of a situation.

Dark Side of 2 (living through ego)

An unbalanced two is co-dependent, uncertain, pessimistic, and hypersensitive when their intuitive self is clouded. Intuition is their main gift and is the center of who they are and how they operate. Whiny, cranky, moody, dualistic, and wishy-washy is the two who has lost their footing within their own energy. A two can buckle under the pressure from stressful or anxiety-ridden situations. As the number of intuition, two is all about going with the flow but at their own pace. They have life lessons that revolve around emotion and intuition so when in the negative, it will often bring about experiences that involve sacrifice and loss in the realm of feeling. Balance can always be re-established through focusing on the intuitive and soulful side of the self where the two belongs.

GREATEST CHALLENGE

Once the intuitive nature of the two becomes clouded, they seek outside themselves for answers creating a co-dependent situation. This is the greatest challenge of the two because it keeps them trapped and reliant on others to makes decisions to navigate life. Their intuitive side is pivotal to their wellbeing and feelings of balance. When it is disconnected, their inner compass is lost. Taking time for self-care and meditation to restore the connection to the intuition is imperative to regaining balance and connection to self.

Soul to Soul Connections

In any relationship, the two is the sensitive and more passive partner. They are there to support and emotionally nourish the other person and are very content to play that role for others. Ironically, even though they are the most feeling and sensitive of all the numbers, pairing with another emotionally based number could prove to be too volatile and unstable. Being more of a passive support system for others, they do better to pair up with natural leaders, thinkers or doers like the one, three, six or nine.

As parents, they are naturally great with children due to their sensitive and intuitive nature. Mothers and fathers who are a two tend to be the favorite parent as they are gentle, loving, and usually not very strict.

Body Talk

Being the most sensitive of the soul plane numbers, the high emotions can lead to nervous anxiety, hypersensitive emotions, and tummy troubles from a lack of grounded energy. When the two is unbalanced, jittery emotions lead to nervous restlessness and touchiness. If emotions run high, the two is high-strung. Re-aligning with the go with the flow intuitive side brings the two back to balance and wholeness. Meditation, listening to soft music, quiet time alone, and spending time in nature are all ways the two can restore balance and equilibrium. The two doesn't work well under pressure and will almost always crumble if things get too intense or stressful.

Path of Service
The two's talents and attributes are best utilized in support roles such as administrative or educational organizations, social work, religious/spiritual roles and artistic endeavors that engage the feeling faculties and are geared more toward guiding than leadership. Anywhere a two can be of support, use their intuitive nature to guide and be a team player, they are content. The key words here are intuitive support.

LIFE THEME NUMBER 5 — "EXPRESSIVE ARTIST"
As the number of the heart and emotions representing freedom of expression, the Life Theme Number five is always looking to be free to express itself. Loathing the nine-to-five grind, they desire flexibility in their schedules both in home and work life. They tend to seek out partners that give them freedom to breathe and express their individuality. At the center of it all, they are essentially the number of the heart. At the core of their desire is to love and be loved.

Called the "Artist's Number," they are naturally gifted in artistic forms such as music, writing, dancing, singing, and acting. Hitler was a Life Theme Number five and was known to have a love for animals as well as be artistically inclined [7].

As much as they seek freedom to express themselves, in the negative they can also seek to control and dominate.

The Life Theme Number 5 energy is loving, sensitive, irregular, artistic, freedom-seeking, passionate, uncertain, power-hungry, dominating, bossy, withdrawn and moody.

Bright Side of 5 (living through spirit)

The Life Theme Number five is the most fun to be with because they are spontaneous, freedom-seeking, and live almost entirely through the realm of feeling. They are unpredictable and live life by how it feels. Heart-centered, they want to create things that stir the soul of others and can often be found in expressive roles like acting, writing, dancing, and less expressive roles like counselor. In their younger years, the need to be free leads them to frequent job, location, and relationship changes. As they mature, their need for freedom to express has to develop some semblance of meaning and direction or their discombobulated way of life will remain chaotic and haphazard, not really achieving any goals.

Dark Side of 5 (living through ego)

Control is the name of the game while a Life Theme Number five is immersed in the negative side of the self. Adolf Hitler showed us all too well that as much as a five can be a loving and artistic energy, it can also have tendencies toward control and domination in an effort to be free to express.

Moodiness is another of the five's dark side traits. If there is something troubling the five, they retreat into isolation to deal with their problem in private. If forced by another to share and consult with others, the person must succumb to the moody wrath of the emotional rollercoaster that is the five energy. I believe that if we could see a five energetic pattern with the naked eye, it would be an erratic up and down pathway as it doesn't like to be in the same place for very long.

The way to balance for a five is to seek out experiences, people and places that allows them to be free to express themselves. Without that, a five will remain restless, agitated, and discontent.

GREATEST CHALLENGE

The five has somewhat of a Dr. Jekyll and Mr. Hyde condition because they can be ultra loving and affectionate as the number of the heart and emotions but are equally as quick to pull away and become cold and distant. The five's greatest challenge is to recognize the importance of finding a balance between the desire for freedom and the need for constructive discipline. Due to their need to be free, the five doesn't always work well with others, and so the development of patience, cooperation and self-control are all major challenges of the five.

Soul to Soul Connections

Relationships are one of the five's demons because they want nothing more than to love and be loved, but, at the same time, they require ample freedom to do their own thing. As a result, more often than not (especially in their younger years) a five tends to subconsciously attract partners that will be emotionally distance and eventually leave them. As they mature, they realize a balance must be reached. Their need for freedom can't override their ability to express love and emotions openly and freely, which goes against their natural nature.

As parents, the five is ultra loving. That feeling of being tied down doesn't seem to apply to their children as it does in intimate relationships. Most fives want a family at some point in their lives because, as the number of the heart and emotions, their desire for love is at the core of who they are. Fives tend to love children and children love them.

Body Talk

The most emotional of all numbers, the heart-centered suffers from pent-up emotion which leads to issues of the heart, blood, and nervous system. As they age, some are emotional bottlers and report issues with high blood pressure, high cholesterol, and heart disease. Naturally empathic like the three, the five tends to hold onto the emotions of others and energetically pick up on emotions that aren't their own and exhibit behaviors linked to those emotions. This is one of the reasons a five can be moody as they work to process and release the emotions. They are bombarded with on a daily basis from external sources.

Allowing a five adequate alone time to sit and process anything that feels out of sorts is the best way to help them regain a sense of balance—mind, body and soul. Remember, their need for freedom to express, whether it is painting a picture or processing emotions, is their natural state of being and will always lead them back to wholeness.

Path of Service
Emotional expression is where it's at for the five. Known as the artist, many fives gravitate toward non-traditional career choices such as acting, singing, dancing, painting, and any other dramatic role. Five is the "balancer" of the soul plane and with the ability to pick up and read emotions, makes a five the natural counselor. They can be found in roles such as school counselor, spiritual guide, teacher, and trainer. Anywhere they can be free to express their views, feelings, and beliefs, such as politics, sales, travel, designing, and so on. Whatever their career choice, they flourish most with a non-traditional schedule where they have adequate freedom to make their own rules. Entrepreneurialism is popular among fives because of the control and freedom it provides. Hard core business, financial, or the structured corporate atmosphere is a no-go for the five and will lead to boredom and frustration very quickly.

LIFE THEME NUMBER 8 — "WISE AND INDEPENDENT LEADER"
Eight is the number of wisdom and independence and anyone carrying this frequency as their Life Theme Number will have an innate desire to guard their ability to be separate in all they do. It is an important part of the eight to feel independent and strong as it

carries an air of assertive, self-assured, and wise energy. As the most active soul plane number, it has a direct link with the realm of spirit affording eight the ability of knowing. Many eights tend to be good in business because they seem to know what to say, when to say it, and how to say it.

Like the five, an eight works best independently. However, in a team atmosphere, others naturally anoint the eight as the leader because they sense their inherent wisdom. Due to their aloof and often emotionally demonstrative nature (as the least sensitive soul plane number), the arena of relationships tends to make up a large portion of their life lessons.

The Life Theme Number 8 energy is independent, wise leader, loving, assertive, confident, dynamic, detached, selfish and cold.

Bright Side of 8 (living through spirit)
The eight is a natural leader, but unlike the nine, which leads with the head, the eight as the most active soul plane number leads with intuition, navigating the situation based on how it feels. As the direct link to spirit, they're dialed in to the greater wisdom of life, having a knack for being knowledgeable in subjects that aren't their area of expertise. Other people naturally gravitate to them for advice and counsel because they instinctively know they have an answer for them. It is their independent drive and undoubting vibe as the confident, assertive, number of wisdom that catapults them into leadership roles in business and otherwise.

Dark Side of 8 (living through ego)
Although the most business savvy and wise of all the numbers, their wisdom falls short when it comes to their own life lessons, which are mostly wrapped up in the connections with others. Their take-charge energy can often make long term friendships a challenge. At the office, they can become the tyrant boss who ruthlessly crushes the hopes and dreams of the weaker links. In other closer relationships,

they are the least emotionally demonstrative of the soul based numbers, which can leave a partner feeling unloved or unwanted.

GREATEST CHALLENGE

The greatest challenge of the eight is to learn that they can still have their independence while forging close relationships. Many eights are plagued with relationship drama until they understand that the security, love, and close connections of a relationship don't detract from their independence. Instead, it adds to it by allowing them the freedom to express their usually reserved or suppressed emotional side.

Soul to Soul Connections

The realm of relationships is where their navigating through feeling and intuition with ease seems to hit a brick wall. In relationships, the eight will immediately pull away if things get too confined or controlling. Independence is the undertone of their life, and when that is threatened or compromised, they become aloof and cold. Like a switch that has been flicked, the eight can become ice cold emotionally, shutting down their heart as the strongest and least sensitive of the soul plane energies.

Interestingly, despite their detached behavior in most relationships, they tend to have a soft heart for children, the ill or the elderly. In these cases, they are more emotionally expressive and loving, that is until their independence becomes jeopardized. As parents, they're either exceptionally lenient and loving or super strict.

Learning to recognize that the love and security of a relationship adds to their life and doesn't take away from it is not only their greatest relationship challenge but their biggest obstacle as a whole.

Body Talk

The eight tend to start out with a strong and healthy physical body when young. Many are athletic or enjoy physical activity as a means of release. As they mature and the reserved emotions begin to build, some succumb to heart and blood related challenges like the five. They are also accident prone, and this is often a subconscious behavior linked to their desire to be loved. The eight is typically a hearty breed that doesn't usually have as many health related challenges as some of the more sensitive numbers. They enjoy a longer life expectancy if things aren't cut short from their accident-ridden tendencies. On a more superficial note, they like to look good and keep up with their appearance on a very regular basis.

Path of Service

Any time they can play the role of ring leader, it is fulfilling to the eight as many do like the spotlight. Due to their naturally confident nature and their desire to be loved, they also don't mind the spotlight and usually bask in it. Business, financial, self-employed, travel, film, and television are just some of the job categories you'll find an eight in. CEO, director, bank manager, teacher, nurse, travel agent, stock broker, and actor are all top choices of the eight, who seeks to put their inherent flowing leadership abilities to work. The more soulfully evolved eight will choose the more expressive and nurturing roles such as nursing or acting. The ones who are still closed down emotionally will tend toward the straight and narrow business and traditional leadership roles like those in the corporate world.

2, 5, 8 — The Physical Plane Numbers

Without the ability to take action, all ideas and inspiration remain in the realm of theory, and we are unable to grow and learn. Our physical bodies are the vehicle through which our soul experiences life for the purpose of learning life lessons. The physical plane energy is the pathway through which our thoughts and ideas manifest into reality. We learn best through doing and experiencing in the physical sense and then processing those experiences through the mind and soul planes for inner growth.

Those lacking or in need of developing the physical energies have a hard time with bringing their ideas to fruition. They often experience frustration from feeling stalled and a sense of being ungrounded.

Taking for granted the physical body and allowing it to become placid or weakened is not healthy as the body is a temple, so to speak. Energy from the mind and soul planes flows downward through the physical body, and if the body is sick, weak, or injured, it impedes proper flow of the energies. We are here to manifest the desires of our soul into the physical realm, and we do that through the use of the physical plane energies. The physical numbers are the anchor for all the other numbers.

LIFE THEME NUMBER 1 — "THE PIONEER AND THE EARTH GUIDE"

As the first physical plane number and the only number that is a stand-alone frequency (can't be divided by any number) it is truly the pioneer that forges its own path. It's the energy with the get up and go—the trailblazing number of new beginnings.

Since it is considered the isolated energy and most associated with the frequency of the ego self, it can be aggressive and become wrapped up in drive and achievement. Those living mostly through the one energy can be unrelenting in their quest to ambitiously achieve their goals.

Those with the one as their Life Theme Number actually carry the "Earth Guide" energy as well since anyone with a date of birth that reduces to one, adds to ten first. Ten literally combines the energies of heaven and earth with the very physical, driven, and aggressive 1 with zero being the symbol of the infinite or spiritual awareness. Many 10/1 people, depending on the individual numbers contained in their birth date, will spend a good portion of their early years living more through the one with only a curiosity for their spiritual side. As they mature, they realize that in order to feel whole and complete, they need to incorporate the other half of their energy. As a guiding frequency, this is a typical timeline for the ten. In order to guide, we must first gain wisdom and knowledge through life experience.

The Life Theme Number 1 energy is verbal self-expression, initiate, action, ambitious, determined, pioneering, aggressive, egocentric and over-driven.

Bright Side of 1 (living through spirit)

As mentioned, the 10/1 will spend the first part of their lives pursuing physical achievement with gusto. Their ambition and drive will take them far into the realm of personal, physical experience. This is necessary for them to pave the way to embrace their true guiding role as the Earth Guide, which is a practical guiding energy that leads through casual conversation. Combining the verbal self-expression number (1) with the spiritual awareness energy, they easily bring forth words of wisdom while sipping a latte with a friend. Most aren't even aware their being guided as a ten isn't preachy or overly spiritual but practical and down to earth. A ten may notice that friends and family will often ask for their advice regularly.

When a ten is in their element and living positively, they are utilizing both sides of their energy (qualities of both one and zero) in roles that allow them to do so. Although ambitious, their drive is usually expressed more through verbal means than in physical exertion. Like cats in the sunshine, the ten likes to keep life light and fun, not delving too deep into the serious problems of life. A ten's preference is to sweep problems under the carpet for another day and enjoy the moment. They do have an eye for aesthetics with great taste when it comes to interior design or choosing fashion and accessories Overall, the ten is adaptable and goes with the flow of life, as that is the way of the pioneer.

Dark Side of 1 (living through ego)
The lopsided ten is living entirely through the detached and driven one. It only wants to associate with those who share the same drive and ambition to rise to the top. The main gift of the ten is their verbal expression, which can make them convincing and persuasive, weaving a tale with their verbal talents to get where they want to be in life. Due to their strong base in the physical, solving problems, whether it is the problems of others or their own, is not something their particularly good at. This can make building strong connections with others difficult for the 10/1 because they avoid dealing with serious issues and challenges.

Greatest Challenge
The greatest challenge of the ten is to learn how to incorporate their spiritual side that is always nudging them and is often considered off limits or taboo. Any number that contains a zero will always have a spiritual depth that can't be denied forever. Many Life Theme Numbers with a zero will deny this part of themselves initially (in younger years) in favor of embracing the traits of whatever other number they're working with (in this case a one). Always curious, their practical and grounded side of the first physical number one keeps their soulful side off limits until they reach a level of maturity that makes them realize they aren't whole and complete without the soul's involvement. Verbally guiding others with their innate spiritual awareness is their birthright yet without drawing upon the soul's wisdom, they can't fulfill their calling.

Soul to Soul Connections
Until they master their softer side, the ten does best in relationships where the other person is also driven for success and achievement. With the development of the zero also comes the ability to connect on a deeper level emotionally. Until that happens, the ten misses the point in relationships and treats them more like a business partnership. Depending on the degree to which they have developed their spiritual

side, some may feel the need to get married, start a family, and set up a home. However, if still young, it is usually more for their desire to build their empire and be involved in the physical nature of life than for the emotional and soulful fulfillment it can provide.

Once the ten balances their physical and soulful energies, they slow down and become great listeners and conversationalists. No longer do they avoid talking through issues and use their gift of verbal expression to keep the relationship communication lines actively open.

As parents, if they have children early, they are more strict and rigid in their parenting style. If they have children when they are older, they are often the go-to parent for advice and guidance. This is not only because they give great advice, but because they know how to have fun too.

Body Talk
When living through the one energy, the unrelenting need to "go" can create feelings of anxiety and restlessness. The ability to truly relax doesn't come easily with so much restless energy. The ten has adaptability as one of their most prized traits, but they never refuse a challenge and would rather be working on achievement than sitting idle. Digestive troubles and muscle tension are common physical afflictions for the ten. Living almost entirely through the physical plane can be tiring on the body, mind, and soul. Meditation can be helpful for the ten to begin engaging the other two planes (soul and mind) and calm the unrelenting mouse wheel of the physical energies.

Path of Service
Any success driven fields such as sales, politics, business, and physical-based roles like sports, interior design, and cooking are a good fit for the ten in their earlier years. As they mature, they begin to desire more meaningful career choices and may gravitate toward things like fundraising, teaching, training, or advice-giving roles. Their innate drive is to guide through verbal means, so they will eventually seek

this out whether it be in their career life or personal life.

LIFE THEME NUMBER 4 — "PRACTICAL DOER"

The four is the doer in every sense of the word. They are practical, loyal, trustworthy, and hard workers not afraid to roll up their sleeves and get in the trenches. They would rather do something than contemplate it, and their one downfall is the contradictory feeling of impatience that many of the fours carry as the steadfast and hardworking balancer of the physical plane energies. They want it all right now and cringe at the thought of working toward a long term goal. Even though they're hard workers, they get easily discouraged by longer time frames to reach achievement.

Sometimes the four can be so practical and grounded that they can restrict their life focus on solely physical or work-related activities. Materialism can also set in and the need to accumulate physical possession can rule them.

The Life Theme Number 4 energy is endurance, progress, foundation, practical, organization, solid, stable, materialistic and impatient.

Bright Side of 4 (living through spirit)

Practical service is the primary pathway of the four. As the number of practicality, organization, and the foundation builder energy, the fours are active doers who are happiest when they are engaged in physical activity that builds in a steady and progressive way. Loyal and trustworthy, they make great business partners and are always a trusted team player.

Preferring the practical to the adventurous or risky, four energy thrives on stability and organization. If you need someone who is great with the small details like the nine does, the four should be your top choice. Hands-on involvement in life keeps the four happy, healthy, and fulfilled.

Dark Side of 4 (living through ego)
While young, the four can be single-focused on their work and creation in the physical realm. As a result they can become overly serious work-a-holics who don't know how to really enjoy life. When this happens, the four neglects the emotional and spiritual side of life such as family, friends, and other meaningful social connections leading to an imbalance of energies. Driven like a work horse creates frustration as ambition and pent up emotions causes the four to present as the irritated party-poopers.

When it comes to matters related to the physical, their lack of patience isn't really evident, but with matters of the realm of relationships, or spiritually based challenges, their patience goes straight out the window. Like the one, engaging in mindful or spiritual practices, such as meditation, goes a long way in rebalancing the energy of the overly grounded four.

GREATEST CHALLENGE
Patience is a virtue, especially for the four. The four has no issue with rolling up their sleeves in the immediate and getting the job done, but when it comes to long term goals and accomplishments (especially those involving the soul's growth), their engine stalls. They become avoiding, whiny, and frustrated. Ironically, the enduring and physical four knows best what hard work can achieve, but they lose interest when it is anything other than purely physical.

Recognizing that some things are worth the long term effort is pivotal to the four's lasting success and happiness.

Soul to Soul Connections
If overly focused on the physical, the four neglects to be actively involved in their relationships, choosing work over socialization and even intimacy with their partner. With a one track focus, pent up anger and frustration is commonly taken out on others around them. They are loyal and reliable partners willing to help in any way they

can, but they often have to work at being sensitive and emotional.

As parents, fours excel in roles like soccer mom or coach. Their parenting style is typically hands-on but often lacks the emotional sensitivity necessary when dealing with children.

Making time for the more meaningful experiences based in the emotional or soulful realm is critical to balancing their energy and maintaining a sense of well being.

Body Talk

Similar to the Life Theme Number one, the four is overly physical to the point that they can develop nerve and stress related conditions from unexpressed emotions. It is important for the four to take time and get in touch with their feelings. They must learn ways to express them openly on a regular basis. If they don't remain mindful of this, it is easy for them to forget and automatically revert back to living purely in the physical realm.

Path of Service

Work that involves the physical, practical, or organization skills of the four is ideal to allow for adequate expression of their strongest attributes. Physical and hands-on careers are top choices for the hard working and physical-based four. Roles such as technicians, tradesperson, chiropractor, and athlete or organizational/practical focused positions as a manager, economist or technical writer are ideal.

LIFE THEME NUMBER 7 — "THE TRUTH SEEKER"

Anyone lucky enough to have a seven in their life knows they often leap before thinking, don't take advice well, and have to have it their way. Even more so than the one and four, the seven is purely physical. The difference is that the seven also forms the base of the Arrow of Spiritual Presence, so there tends to be a spiritual depth present (whether actively tapped or not) that can be drawn out and expanded upon.

Called the teaching/learning number, the seven learns almost entirely through personal experience, usually involving sacrifice, loss and/or hardship to some degree. It is a blessing in disguise for the seven as they learn a tremendous amount in a short period of time leading to them taking a quantum leap in their soul's development. Even though they go through experiential boot camp in their early life, racking up heartache and loss regularly, they become the wise sages later in life, able to share what they've learned. Reviewing their life's stories with others is the optimum means of learning.

Many younger sevens will say that it seems as though life has dealt them a bum deal. Repeating and attracting of the same hurtful patterns and experiences is common. Older sevens will count their blessings for a full life with much learned in a short amount of time.

The Life Theme Number 7 energy is wise, contemplative, achiever, truth-seeking, determined, stubborn, active, distrustful, and hesitant.

Bright Side of 7 (living through spirit)
As the deep philosophical number, the happy seven is one that is free to experience a balance of emotional engagement and release and intellectual stimulation.

As natural healers, sevens like to use their hands to teach and guide. They are in their element when they are sharing with others the wisdom and knowledge they've gleaned from their never-ending stream of accumulating life experiences. They are essentially people-oriented folks who desire to be involved in the physical parts of life. They like to both show and tell.

Less talk more action is the motto of the seven, but when asked about their own life, they turn into incredible storytellers with much wisdom to share. Sharing of their life experiences is also a great way to release building emotions that the seven typically carries.

Dark Side of 7 (living through ego)

Like the four, they are almost entirely physical based which causes them to put the blinders on their emotional and spiritual self. This makes it harder to recognize and correct repeating patterns that don't serve their highest good. Rebellion is one of the biggest challenge areas for the seven. Whenever someone tries to tell them what is right for them, even if they know it's the right thing, they run in the opposite direction. From my personal experience with clients, many children who have been diagnosed with oppositional defiance disorders have the seven either as their Life Theme Number or carry multiple sevens on their birth chart. Like the ADHD children who tend to carry multiple nines, it is another interesting pattern to pay close attention to.

When a seven is living in the negative, they are rebellious, entirely in physical mode (detached emotionally), and repeatedly attract experiences that bring about learning through hindsight. Life is much harder than it needs to be for the unbalanced seven. Of all the numbers, life can get hairy fast when the seven is not utilizing the emotions or the mind plane to assimilate and integrate the stream of live-and-learn lessons constantly coming at them from every angle.

GREATEST CHALLENGE

The seven is a hindsight learner until they recognize the patterns they continue to repeatedly attract and live out. Their greatest challenge is to recognize the patterns they are attracting that cause them to repeat hurtful lessons. Although it is their nature to learn through personal experience, which usually involves some degree of hindsight learning, some sevens suffer more and longer than others to learn the same lessons. It can end up feeling like a merry-go-round, and the seven can get comfortable with life always being hard, not recognizing the fact that life doesn't have to be so difficult.

Soul to Soul Connections

The seven attracts patterns that involve hardship in the three areas of life: relationships, health, and finances. Since they aren't particularly emotional based, they don't do well with judging the character and motives of others. This leads them to attract partners who don't have their best interests at heart, which in turn leads to more hindsight learning.

As parents, their non-conforming rebellious ways and their need for adequate alone time can make adjusting to the role of parent tough. As with the four, the seven also parents from a hands-on learning and teaching style. As the truth seeker energy, has the added deeper element of wanting to encourage the child to find their truth and live it.

Body Talk

Like all the physical based numbers, the seven has a harder time with emotional expression resulting in pent up feelings. When things get too intense, the seven will close down and tune out, retreating back into the world of the physical. Lacking the practical energy that the four has, the seven is even more prone to releasing built up emotions in an explosive manner. As the base of both the Arrow of Practical Action and the Arrow of Great Expression which we'll explore further in chapter six, the seven carries a great deal of restless energy to start with.

Aside from restless energy, repeatedly being burned in relationships (hindsight learning) can cause the seven to accumulate a massive amount of emotional energy. Releasing feelings through physical exertion is one of the best ways for the seven to relieve the impending emotional volcanic eruption. The seven has a leg up on the four because the seven also likes adequate alone time to mindfully reflect on their experiences. If a seven seems frazzled or overwhelmed, the best course of action is to encourage or allow them to retreat into isolation for self-reflection and re-centering.

Path of Service

The seven loves to work with their hands and their energy flows most strongly through their palms. They are drawn to shiny tools such as scissors, scalpels, and other metallic instruments and do well in positions that allow them to be hands-on. Hairstylists, surgeons, butchers, artists, healers, and carpenters are just some of the roles you'll find a seven engaged in. On the flip side, they are also the deep and philosophical truth-seekers who edge toward roles that fulfill this calling such as philosopher, teacher, counselor, scientist, and lawyer. They love to teach and guide others and any role that satisfies this desire is a great choice.

You now have the knowledge to understand the main energetic essence of not only yourself but everyone in your life too. To know this one number can shift your perspective entirely. What you thought was a nagging wife, a tuned out husband, or a difficult child is really a mental based woman, a physical based man, and a soul based child. Discovering this single piece of knowledge about the people in your life can help you overcome many relationship challenges.

As a numerologist, I can frequently be found scribbling the birth dates of those I meet on napkins at restaurants or scrap pieces of paper from my purse. To me, it is one of the most effective ways to discover who I am interacting with and how to relate to them.

If you have others in your life that you just don't get on one level or another, start here with the Life Theme Number as it will show you the essence of who they truly are.

CHAPTER 5: YOUR DATE OF BIRTH IS THE RECIPE OF YOUR LIFE

Each Number in Your Date of Birth Is an Ingredient in the Recipe of YOU

According to the science of numerology, the individual numbers in your date of birth is similar to DNA only it's the coding of our soul. Instead of telling us we'll have brown hair and blue eyes, it shows us that we need to work on communicating our emotions, develop our creative energy, or that we have a knack for naturally counseling others. These things could take us decades to discover but can be revealed in an instant through the coding of our date of birth. It reveals the energetic patterns we have to work with. The Birth Chart is one of the most important interpretative pieces in the system of numerology and numbers.

THE BIRTH CHART

The empty Pythagorean Birth Chart symbolizes the soul prior to incarnation. In essence, it is our blank drawing board upon which we sketch out our life. The Birth Chart is drawn like a tic-tac-toe diagram. Each row represents one of the three planes of existence—the mind, soul, and physical planes. Comparing it to the human body, the top row is the head, the middle row is the heart/soul, and the bottom row is the lower body/leg area.

Mind Plane			
Soul Plane			
Physical Plane			

Each base number from one to nine has its own permanent location on the birth chart. The birth chart filled out in its entirety looks like this:

Mind Plane	3	6	9
Soul Plane	2	5	8
Physical Plane	1	4	7

Of course, no birth date has all the base numbers present. If that were the case, the birth chart would be fully balanced with no lesson areas (missing numbers), and there would be no need for you to be here on Earth. A birth date can contain up to eight numbers, but only seven of the nine unique base numbers. The number one, two or three are frequently repeated in many birth dates. This leaves at least two or more blank spaces (missing numbers), and whenever there are empty spaces, this indicates our lesson areas.

We are born with some of the base numbers present already, but the aim is to develop the qualities of all the base numbers one to nine, striving to build the completed and balanced birth chart, with all numbers present. For example, if your birth date is missing the numbers two, five and seven, these are your main lesson areas in this lifetime. You need to work on developing and integrating the qualities and attributes of those numbers. As we move through our lives and gain in maturity, we will all automatically develop our missing qualities, through life experience. However, knowing what's on the lesson plan is more fun and rewarding, giving us the creative power to shape our destiny as we desire.

COMPLETING YOUR BIRTH CHART

Using the birth date of May 18, 1975, the diagram below illustrates what this birth date looks like when written on the birth chart:

Mind Plane			9
Soul Plane		55	8
Physical Plane	11		7

Using your own birth date, fill in your own birth chart. If you have multiples of the same digit simply place them in the same space side by side, as shown above with the double ones and double fives. Remember, each base number has its own permanent space as shown here:

Mind Plane	3	6	9
Soul Plane	2	5	8
Physical Plane	1	4	7

ANALYZING YOUR BIRTH CHART

Now that you have your pretty little tic-tac-toe diagram filled out with your birth date digits, it is time to find out what it means to you. We've already examined the nine base numbers and the qualities of each, but what does it mean to have two ones, three fives or missing the number four? There are many potential combinations, and the world is full of interesting people to prove it. Let's discover the traits, tools, and lessons areas you have hidden within your date of birth.

The sections to follow discusses the nine base number meanings in more detail, giving definitions of what it means to have single, multiple, isolated, or missing base numbers on your birth chart. Look first at the meanings of the numbers present on your chart (traits/tools) and then continue on to examine the meanings of the missing numbers (lesson areas) on your birth chart.

Typically, the most balanced form of the nine base numbers is in their singular form. The rule of thumb is, the more multiples, the more the negative qualities of that number are amplified. Although the numbers present on our birth chart represent our tools, excessive multiples of numbers can represent challenges with those tools. For example, having a single two can give us a solid intuitive sense and emotional sensitivity, but triple twos can take those sensitivities to an almost unbearable level unless we understand how to work with those excessive energies.

THE BASE NUMBERS IN SINGULAR FORM
The Most Balanced Expression of a Number

Single 1 – Most numbers work best alone, but the single one is the exception. The one, being a very ego-based energy, can isolate itself easily from the other numbers. This detachment creates difficulty in expressing the emotions and the inner self. Speaking is not usually a problem for the single one because the ego has much to say. However, when it comes to expressing true feelings, the single one finds matching feelings with the appropriate words challenging.

Single 2 – As the number of intuition and sensitivity, the two in singular form gives an average intuitive sense and a balanced emotional sensitivity. The single two is not overly sensitive and has just the right amount of gut instinct. Emotions are typically more balanced with a single two, and hypersensitivity is usually not a concern. However, if there is a single two on a woman's chart, it can seem more like double two as woman are generally more empathically intuitive by nature.[8]

Single 3 – Three is the number of imagination and memory, and so it is no surprise that those who possess one on their birth chart are mental keeners. A great memory, vivid imagination, and mental stamina are available to the single three. The mind is a tool to be used and put away when not needed. It is not meant to be relentlessly on autopilot as seen with the multiple three.

Single 4 – Four is the most solid, stable, and grounded of all numbers. It gives the birth chart a good footing in physical reality to balance an overactive mind or sensitive emotions. Four is the what-you-see-is-what-you-get number. It is practical, honest, and forthright, bringing balance to anything over the top. As the middle Physical Plane number, four is heavily anchored in the materialistic and tangible side of life.

Single 5 – The middle birth chart number has an important job to do. Five represents the heart and emotions. It links all the other birth chart numbers together through its location in the center of the chart. Five symbolizes love and emotional expression, and when it comes to numbers, it is possible to have too much of a good thing. Emotional control is important for our wellbeing and social success. The single five creates a good balance of emotional expression and control—emotions and moods are even keeled. Feelings are a guide and not a handicap with the single five.

Single 6 – Six being the number of extremes, the singular form of the six is definitely best. Six is the balancer, nurturer, and martyr of the mind plane with an emphasis on responsibility. As the number of creativity, it can also bring that spark of excitement and wonder to the mental sphere. However, the single six has a tendency to allow its domestic side to dominate, preferring to concentrate creative energy within the home as the responsible domestic goddess. An extra push may be needed for the single six to use those same creative juices on a grander scale in the form of creative expression for the greater good, the true purpose of the six.

Single 7 – Seven is the teaching/learning number, and those who have one on their chart will no doubt get a good helping of personal experience. The seven prefers to learn through hindsight, which is why sacrifice and/or loss tends to be a part of seven's learning curve. The seven leaps before looking and usually pays for it later. Life usually isn't boring when there is a seven on the birth chart. As the most active number on the physical plane, the emphasis is on learning through doing in a physical sense. All this "doing" may involve some heartache and loss, but the abundance of personal experience is meant to allow for the rapid accumulation of wisdom and knowledge, which is the goal of the seven.

Single 8 – Eight has guts. It is the most confident and assertive of all numbers. When a single eight is present on a birth chart, it can give that extra push needed to go after a goal and achieve it. A single eight is just the right combination—too many eights and guts turns into fearlessness, which may or may not be a good thing. When a single eight energy is not used, it can lead to pent up energy and restless behavior. The independent energy of the eight needs appropriate avenues of expression or it paces in its cage, becoming moody and reactive. Eight is the number of wisdom yet, it cannot gain wisdom if it is not allowed to be free. Mentally dominant people have the hardest time utilizing the confident and assertive eight energy, yet these are the very people who could use it that most.

Single 9 – Ambitious, idealistic, and opinionated, a single nine brings a healthy dose of opposition to any conversation. Nine is the big thinker, the leader and the justice-seeking humanitarian. Unlike the six, nine will not stand for playing the role of doormat. Nine's powerful energy is best in the singular to allow the other numbers room to express themselves. The nine thinks in terms of black and white, right and wrong, and they can get carried away with needing to be right. Generally, the more nines, the more rigid and idealistic the thinking becomes. Nine is the very reason why, during the past 100+ years, we've seen such progress and achievement in all areas of civilization. Every birth date in the twentieth century had at least one nine!

MULTIPLES OF THE SAME NUMBER
The Unbalanced Version of a Number

It is very common for a birth date to contain at least one multiple of the base numbers one to nine. Whenever a base number appears as a multiple, the rule of thumb is that the traits of the number are exaggerated, usually in a more negative way. For most numbers, the most balanced representation of the number is in singular form. Any more than one of any number can create a top-heavy scenario where the traits of that number dominants the birth chart. Typically, the more multiple of the same number, the more it dominants, turning an asset into a liability.

Multiple 1 – The most balanced expression of the one is in double form. Not all numbers are better in pairs, but this is the case with the one. Double ones add to two, and with this undertone of two energy, the one is better able to balance ego with the cooperative and sensitive energies of the two. Thus, the double ones give a balanced expression of their unique quality which is the ability to easily express verbally. Using the sensitive energy of the two, are able to share their inner feelings more easily. More than two ones and we see a reverting back to the meaning of a single one, with difficulty in expressing inner sensitivities. Typically, with three or more ones we see the chatterbox syndrome with the excessive amount of verbal energy. Yet, despite their talkative nature, expression of their inner feelings is still difficult.

Multiple 2 – Intuition and sensitivity is an important factor in successful social interaction. We use our gut instincts all the time to read between the lines—only 10% of human communication is verbal![9] When two or more twos are present on a birth chart, gut instinct can turn into hypersensitivity. With this degree of sensitivity, intuition often becomes clouded by heightened emotions and too much energetic clutter. Multiple twos bestow exceptional intuitive ability and spiritual sensitivity, but the radio signal is usually full of static. As a psychic sponge, it is easy to become overwhelmed intuitively and emotionally.

Multiple 3 – A vivid imagination is a wonderful thing, but there is something to the saying, *don't let your imagination run away with you.* The three is the motor of the mind plane, and it can very easily overheat if revved too high. This is exactly what happens when there are two or more threes present on a birth chart. The already hyperactive mental energy of the three, which is quick-witted and computer-like in mental precision and speed, goes into overdrive when in multiple form. Ideas can begin to lack logic and reality can slip out of reach. Many with multiple threes are misunderstood because they can become lost in their own world. They do, however, make excellent writers and usually express themselves best in written form.

Multiple 4 – The emphasis of the four energy is very much on the physical plane with its grounded, practical, and down-to-earth energy. However, in multiple form, the four can become obsessed with all things physical. Materialism can take hold, taking the four from honest and hardworking to co-dependent and greedy.

Experiencing life for the sake of material and tangible pleasures can be like a drug to the multiple four. It is an ever-present lure for the plural four to live just on the surface of life where things are fun and easy. This can be avoided by remembering to incorporate activities that draw upon the inner self, such as meditation or volunteer work.

Multiple 5 – Like the multiple two, the multiple five brings hypersensitivity. However, the sensitivity of the multiple five is focused mainly on the emotions. In the singular, five is open, loving, and in control of emotions. In the plural, five is emotionally guarded and has to feel safe in order to express emotions. Those with multiple fives are "emotional bottlers," stuffing emotions inside instead of openly dealing with them. They have a sensitive heart and are very loving and compassionate, but they have a hard time dealing with emotional trauma, so they prefer not to. Denial is the multiple five's favorite weapon against emotional turmoil.

Multiple 6 – The multiple six loves to play the "what-if" game. Any mental number in multiple form is gifted with an abundance of mind power, but when this excess brain wave energy is not actively and positively used, it slips into useless mind-chatter mode. Creativity in the negative forms destructive thought patterns. Drama seems to follow the multiple six, and life can seems harder than it really is. Nagging, whining, complaining, and over-exaggerating things way out of proportion are warning signs that the multiple six has taken a tumble into the black abyss. There is enormous creative potential present with more than one six, but using it wisely is the challenge.

Multiple 7 – Seven is the teaching/learning number, and much of this learning comes in the form of hindsight through sacrifice and/or loss. When there is more than one seven on a birth chart, it becomes an accelerated learning program. Typically, the more sevens, the more likely that similar experiences involving some form of loss will be repeated before the lesson is fully learned. Repeatedly attracting the wrong relationships, continually making unsuitable career choices, or making spur of the moment choices that bring regret later are all typical for this number. The multiple seven may seem like a bum deal, but it is meant to bring about rapid learning for the sake of gaining wisdom and knowledge. Those with multiple sevens have a bigger purpose later in life related to sharing their wealth of wisdom and knowledge with others. They become the wise sages, drawing upon their tremendous amount of personal experience to teach others about life. Multiple sevens usually equates to a fairly turbulent early life, but all that suffering leads to an accumulation of a wealth knowledge and wisdom in a shorter amount of time.

Multiple 8 – Energetically, the multiple eight is a bit of a daredevil energy. Eight is confident, assertive, and independent energy, but when the eight appears as a pair or more, confidence turns to boldness. When a birth chart has two or more eights there can be restlessness within, and a need to continually drum up experiences for the sake of the experience. These people get rather bored by the mundane, and they usually don't shy away from trying something new. Eight is a unique soul plane number because it is the only "feeling" number linked to the "doing" energy of the four (four is half of eight). Going after a goal is definitely not difficult for the multiple eight energy— they'll try anything once (or twice).

Multiple 9 – Although nine is a three-part number of ambition, idealism, and responsibility, when nine appears in multiples, idealism takes center stage. Those with two or more nines are excellent at thinking big, creating a mental vision of what they want to achieve, and then going after it with gusto. However, their visions aren't always the most realistic or workable in real life, and the more nines, the more out in left-field their ideas seem to be. Attention to detail isn't the nine's strong suit like it is for the practical four. This is exactly why the multiple nine's inspired plans seem to hit so many stumbling blocks The nine is much better with the bigger picture, but a good plan of action needs both the outline and the minor details hammered out. Anyone with more than one nine can become extremely mentally dominant, living in the mental sphere most of the time. Regularly engaging in activities that involve the lower two planes (soul and physical) is necessary to keep a balanced outlook.

THE ISOLATED NUMBERS
Overcoming the Challenges of the Blocked Energies of 1, 3, 7 and/or 9.

An isolated number is a number that is trapped in the corner of the birth chart, cut off from the other numbers (the numbers surrounding it are missing). The only numbers that can become isolated are the one, three, seven and nine because these are the numbers in the four corners of the birth chart. When a number becomes trapped or isolated, the energy of that number is unable to flow and integrate with the other numbers. The other numbers are unable to communicate with the isolated number and vice versus causing ideas to become trapped in the mind or experiences to be repeated over and over again. It is similar to having a telephone conversation through a static-filled line. Only part of the conversation is heard, creating miscommunications and misunderstandings. To bridge the gap between numbers, developing the qualities of the nearby missing numbers are essential to create an outlet for the trapped energy. In order for an idea to be brought to life, we must be able to experience it on all three levels—mind, body and soul.

Isolated 1 - When the one has no other numbers surrounding it on the birth chart, there is a tendency to isolate itself even more than usual. The number of ego expression has no problem detaching itself from the other numbers, and so we see further withdrawal from speaking true feelings and expressing from a soul level. Those with an isolated one avoid speaking about how they feel because they are so often misunderstood when they attempt to communicate their feelings. Developing the qualities of the two, four, and/or five will help to free up the isolated one energy, allowing for easier communication of the inner feelings.

Isolated 3 – Three is the number of imagination, and when our imagination is cut off from the rest of our qualities, we can't implement our ideas easily. Ideas remain just ideas with no easy avenue of expression. Frustration can occur from having such a vivid imagination, by experiencing difficulty successfully and acting on those thoughts. Developing the qualities of the two, five and/or six will help to free up the isolated three energy, allowing ideas to be utilized instead of wasted.

Isolated 7 – Here's where the seven's abundance of personal experience turns from interesting to a bit ugly. Seven frequently learns through hindsight, but when the seven is isolated, the lesson isn't always learned the first time around. The ability to assimilate and integrate the lesson is not there because the seven is cut off from the other two planes (soul and physical). The seven is a bit slow to get the joke. The same mistakes are repeatedly made, and "bad luck" seems to follow those with an isolated seven. For the isolated seven, repeated lessons are even more accentuated than those of multiple sevens. Developing the qualities of the four, five and/or eight will help to break the cycle of repeated misfortune experienced by the isolated seven energy.

Isolated 9 – What could be more frustrating for the ambitious and idealistic nine energy than having a big idea that can't be acted upon? Nothing! When one or more nines are isolated on a birth chart, this is exactly what happens—big ideas are plentiful, but there are no outlets for them. They tend to act out their excess mental energy in the form of criticism and opinions because these "ideas" don't have an avenue for physical expression. Those with isolated nines can get stuck in a world of fantasy, living out their ideas only in their mind. Developing the qualities of the five, six, and/or eight can help to release the pent up ambition and idealism of the isolated nine energy.

Developing a self-awareness regarding areas of growth allows us to utilize the traits/tools our numbers give us. For example, if you're missing the number four (which is the practical, grounded foundation number), but you have double nines, (the number of idealism and ambition), you aren't likely to be great with the finer details but are a big dreamer. With the energy of the double nines, you can focus that drive, determination, and visionary thinking on building the more practical/foundational energy of the missing four. In doing so, you not only fill in the blank and develop the missing qualities of the four, but you also ground the over-the-top thinking of the double nine energy in the process. It's a double whammy.

To fully understand your complete essence, you need to have both sides of the equation, which includes your strengths and weaknesses. You know what tools you have to work with, now let's find out how you're going to use those tools to fill in the missing blanks and step into wholeness.

Now that you've had an in-depth view of the tools and traits you possess, as well as some of the challenges that can come along with those frequencies in excess or isolation, the next chapter will put a spotlight on your challenge areas or areas of development represented by the missing numbers or blank spaces on the birth chart.

CHAPTER 6: DEFINING YOUR STRENGTHS & WEAKNESSES

Knowing Your Talents and Handicaps Can Mean
the Difference Between Frustration and Fruition

One of the greatest epiphanies I had when I first fell in love with the numbers was the moment I revealed my strengths and weaknesses. It explained so much … why I tended to be a people-pleaser, and why I suffered from restless anxiety. I discovered my ailments weren't because of any medical condition, but they were due to the fact that I had all three of the most active numbers on the birth chart and all three of the physical plane numbers too. Not to mention that I struggled with emotional expression—not because I was cold or insensitive but because I was lacking the sensitive frequencies.

On the flip side, I also discovered that my unrelenting need to *just do it* as the Nike slogan says, wasn't only an inability to be able to truly relax but was one of my prized traits and the main catalyst in much of my success in life.

All of these things I confirmed about myself through not only examining the numbers I had in my date of birth, which represents the tools/traits we are born with, but also taking a closer look at the numbers I was missing too. These missing energies represent our challenge areas where we need to fill in the blanks. They are energies we need to bring in some much needed balance to the numbers we already carry. We are here to learn and grow through our life experiences, which brings us closer to a whole, complete and balanced soul.

THE MISSING NUMBERS
Our Life Lessons Mapped Out

Just to refresh your memory, the numbers present on our birth chart are the tools/traits we possess, and the missing numbers (blank spaces) represent our lesson areas. These are your weaker areas in need of effort for growth. Think of them as your lesson areas in this lifetime. The goal is to develop a balanced expression of the qualities of all the base numbers one to nine.

However, as we have read in the multiple and isolated numbers sections, the missing numbers on our chart are not the only area that needs improvement or development. Sometimes our best qualities can be both our gift and our curse, depending upon how we utilize them. Numbers, like perfume scents, are best in moderation otherwise they can be overwhelming.

Missing 1 – No one born in the twentieth century can be missing this number as all birth years in the previous century began with one. Since the turn of the century, the one has been replaced by the two which makes missing a one much more common. As the number that governs communication, the missing one poses some challenges in verbal self-expression. Two, as the number of intuition and sensitivity, has now replaced the one as the first number in any birth year and so we are seeing a shift from verbal communication toward more non-verbal avenues. One represents verbal expression (ego) and two represents non-verbal expression (soul). Children born in year 2000 or later have at least one two, which automatically gives them heightened extra-sensory perception. Telepathic communication is very common amongst the newest generation. Children missing a one can seem quiet and non-verbal, but this is no stranger than someone with four ones who is a chatter-box. This is simply their energetic make-up, and forcing them to perform verbally would be going against their natural inclinations.

Missing 2 – As the number of intuition and sensitivity, birth dates lacking a two indicate the tendency toward being a bit out of touch with the intuitive self. Gut instinct usually isn't the first response for those missing the two. They can certainly be sensitive and deeply feeling people, but when it comes to trusting their own instincts or intuition, they get wishy-washy. The realm of the mind is usually their home-base in terms of decision-making. When it comes to intuition, practice makes perfect. Actively and consciously relying on the intuitive faculties more frequently can develop those missing two qualities and bring some much needed balance. Our mind can be a great tool, but sometimes you've just got to go with your gut.

Missing 3 – Three is the energizer bunny of the Mind Plane. Imaginative and as sharp as a tack, the three energy keeps the mental sphere in tip-top shape. When the three is absent on the birth chart, mental laziness and poor memory can develop. Mental laziness is less likely if there is an abundant quantity of the other mental numbers (six and nine) but poor memory or "selective" memory tends to be a constant symptom of the missing three. Exercising the mental faculties is imperative to keep the mind in top form. The phrase "use it or lose it" certainly fits here.

Missing 4 – Impractical sums up the missing four. As the number of practicality, organization, and stability, the energy of the four keeps us grounded with our ideas and actions, sprinkling a dash of sound practical reasoning on everything we do. Without a four, mind plane energies can slip, and physical plane energies tend to jump with both feet. The four is like the anchor on our boat; it keeps us from drifting too far. Those missing a four can be a tad irrational and tend to skip minor, yet important, details. As the number of steady step-by-step progress, absence of the four can mean becoming easily annoyed and impatient with difficult people or situations. Patience is a virtue.

Missing 5 – When the five is present, there is emotional balance, open expression of love and compassion, and some protection from emotional hypersensitivity. When the five is missing, the opposite tends to be the case. Those missing a five feel as though expressing love and compassion openly to anyone is out of their element. They generally aren't the touchy-feely type, preferring to reserve their loving expression for those they are most comfortable with. Developing the qualities of the five is similar to breaking in new shoes. It takes time and repeated use for it to comfortably fit. When it comes to matters of the heart, we all have our own unique expression.

Missing 6 – Unless there is also an imaginative three present, the missing six means more effort is needed to develop the creative side. When the creative spunk associated with the six is lacking, it may be more difficult to see the bigger vision of things. Six is not just about acting on an idea it is about capturing a complete vision and living it out it its entirety. This is true creativity. Start by using the visionary six energy with small creative endeavors, and begin applying those newly learned visionary skills to bigger, bolder goals and dream.

Missing 7 – Personal experience for the purpose of gaining wisdom and knowledge is the path of the seven energy. When seven is missing on a birth chart, it doesn't necessarily mean there is a lack of personal experience, but it does mean that the ability to learn from those experiences the first time around is hindered. Since sevens usually learn the hard way, through sacrifice and loss, it is a wise and philosophical number. When the seven is missing, it may be harder to fully grasp and appreciate the deeper meaning behind the experiences.

Missing 8 – Eight is a gutsy, confident, wise, and independent energy. When the eight is missing, reserved behaviors can hinder achievement. As the number of wisdom, eight's undercurrent of intuitive "knowing" can give a self-assured feeling that you're headed in the right direction. Without the eight, indecisiveness and lack of confidence can let the air out of the balloon. The missing eight scenario is a good opportunity to practice spontaneity and risk-taking—in moderation of course.

Missing 9 – Like the one, all birth dates in the twentieth century have at least one nine. The newer generations are experiencing the absence of the ambitious and idealistic nine energy. The nine is the most driven and forceful of the mind plane numbers. It is fiery and determined to the point of pigheadedness. When the nine is missing, there is typically less drive for achievement in the physical sense. Those without a nine are more inclined to be *at* peace rather than fight *for* peace. Caution should be exercised when attempting to develop the missing nine qualities—a little dab will do.

ARROWS OF PYTHAGORAS
Defining our Strengths and Challenges

The old adage is true; there *is* strength in numbers. If you have three blank spaces in a row or three numbers in a row on a birth chart, it accentuates the power of those energies. Three blank spaces highlight and emphasize a cluster of weaker areas needing further development while three numbers in a row combines the talents and energies of all the numbers forming a unified and stronger strength area.

When the numbers (or blank spaces) join in a row on a birth chart, similar to the game tic-tac-toe, they are called arrows. The Arrows of Pythagoras are a part of the work of the Greek philosopher, Pythagoras (the "Father of Numerology").[10]

As we have learned, the numbers on our birth chart represent our strengths and the missing numbers represent our developmental or weakness areas.

The head of the arrow typically points toward the strongest of the three numbers with this number acting as the leader of the pack. The exception to the rule is if there are multiple numbers within an Arrow. For example, the numbers one, five, nine form the Arrow of Determined Effort with the head of the arrow at the ambitious, idealistic, and responsible nine. If there were double ones present, the strength of the arrow would be redirected away from the nine and refocused on the ones, which is the number of verbal self-expression (communication). The determination of this arrow's energy would be refocused on more verbal expression of determination, such as voicing an opinion or being the voice of a movement.

A birth chart may have many arrows or no arrows at all. Regardless of how many you have, your Arrows of Pythagoras (or absence of) can put your strengths and areas in need of growth under the microscope for a clearer view, bringing even more clarity and understanding into your life.

ARROWS OF STRENGTH
Strength in Numbers (3 numbers in a row)

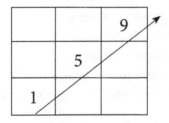

Arrow of Determined Effort (1, 5, 9)
The power and strength of this arrow is contained within the ambitious and idealistic nine. As a natural leader, nine draws out

the pioneering energies of the one and the expressive energies of the five to create an arrow full of drive and determination. Nine is the humanitarian number, so the ambitious and idealistic drive of this arrow is meant for good. However, with the idealistic thinking of the nine energy leading the team and forging full steam ahead, missing the mark entirely is commonplace. The stubborn pigheadedness of this arrow can cause a wrong turn to go unrecognized for longer than necessary. Everything we set our sights on is not necessarily meant for us. Knowing when to change gears or direction, if necessary, is the key to harnessing the power of this arrow. While blindsided by such driving force, you really can't see the forest for the trees.

Keywords: Drive, ambition, determination, stubborn, willful, strong-minded, idealistic.

Arrow of Great Expression (7, 8, 9)

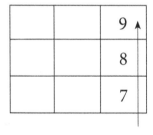

As the title of this arrow indicates, there is great potential for expression when the power of the most active numbers on each the three planes of existence join forces. Present within this trinity is the ambitious and idealistic drive of the nine, the wise, assertive, and independent energy of the eight, and the insatiable urge of the seven to learn through personal experience. This is an unstoppable combination of energies that can lead to limitless potential. The down side of this arrow is that when not in active use, the merged energies of the nine, eight, and seven can create restlessness and hyperactivity. Regular rest and relaxation, away from the stresses of life, is essential to release pent up energy and avoid feeling overwhelmed. Crowds, technological devices, big cities, and other highly stimulating things should be kept to a minimum, choosing instead outdoor activities in nature. Many people who have changed the world in big ways have this arrow on their birth chart. Einstein, Nelson Mandela, and Napoleon Bonaparte are just a few examples of the potential power of the Arrow of Great Expression.

Keywords: **Drive, ambition, expressive, achievement, limitless potential, unstoppable, nervousness, restlessness.**

Arrow of Spiritual Presence (3, 5, 7)

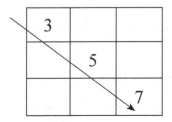

Those who hold the combined power of the three, five, and seven are said to have an air of peace and calm surrounding them. The Dalai Lama has this combination, and many have noted this feeling while in his presence. The peacefulness associated with this arrow is created by the ease of which those with this combination learn and integrate experiences. In order to fully appreciate and learn from an experience, we must be able to live it on all three levels of existence—we need to mentally assess it, feel it, and physically experience it. This arrow joins the mentally sharp and imaginative energy of the three with the compassionate and love centered five and the deeply philosophical and physically driven seven. In essence, the three, five, and seven are the most powerfully expressive energies of the three planes. This combination produces an innate spiritual awareness, which is the root of their peaceful presence. There is an underlying and ever-present feeling of trust that all is well, despite the direst of circumstances. It is interesting to note that those born in the last century who has the Arrow of Spiritual Presence on their birth chart also have the Arrow of Determined Effort. These arrows seem very contradictory. Indeed, the drive and determination of the Arrow of Determined Effort can overshadow the qualities of the Arrow of Spiritual Presence. In the present century, as peace begins to dominant the energies of the planet with the replacement of the nine for the two in every birth date, the Arrow of Spiritual Presence will shine alone for the first time in over 100 years.

Keywords: Peace, calm, gentle, loving, understanding, trusting, serenity, spiritually aware, truth-seeker.

Arrow of Practical Action (1, 4, 7)

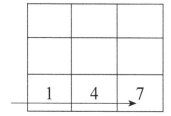

When all three Physical Plane numbers join forces, there is an intense drive for physical expression and experience. As the doers of society, they aren't content unless they're involved in the physical aspects of life. Not really the theoretical thinkers (unless their Life Theme Number is a mental one), but rather the risk-takers who aren't afraid to use some elbow grease. Anyone with the Arrow of Practical Action knows that it takes physical effort to manifest any goal. These people live for the exhilaration of the obstacles and challenges of life, but the secret to their success is that they approach things in a practical, grounded, and realistic way. Challenge them to the seemingly impossible and they'll be eager to prove you wrong. Their strength, resilience, and stamina are quite admirable.

However, there is a tendency with this numerical combination to slip into the material aspects of the physical plane. This is especially so if their Life Theme Number is also one of the physical plane numbers one, four, or seven. When materialism takes hold, physical expression is for the sake of physical pleasure, often in the form of material possessions or superficial experiences. Overindulgence in food, sex, drugs, shopping, or gambling can all be common addictive lures with such an abundance of physical energy. Actively working toward meaningful goals and challenges keep the superficial side of the physical numbers at bay.

The human body is a tool meant to assist us in the expression of our true (spiritual) self. It is very easy for those with all three physical plane numbers to bring their ideas to reality in the physical "doing" sense. When all three physical energies are present and active, the spiritual force has a firm and grounded footing in the physical plane, which makes for ease of spiritual expression in this dense, Earthly realm. Of course not everything will work out perfectly 100% of the time, but at least you can't blame them for not putting in the effort. The saying, "If at first you don't succeed, try, try again" was probably written about a person who has the Arrow of Practical Action.

Keywords: Practical, useful, helpful, stamina, resilient, hard-working, solid, stable, grounded, down-to-earth, active, doer.

Arrow of Mental Power (3, 6, 9)

3	6	9

The phrase "ignorance is bliss" doesn't apply here. When all three mental plane numbers come together it is like connecting the dots. These folks are mental keeners with a mind like a computer. They're quick to assess a person or situation and are able to read between the lines easily. Nothing much gets past them. They rarely seem lost for words, have endless ideas and solutions to problems, and integrate new information at the speed of light. However, mental giftedness comes with big burdens. Over-thinking, over-analyzing, and mental burn out are common scenarios for people with this number combination. The motor has a hard time winding down—even for sleep.

Many would envy those with such above average mental talents, but being mentally dominant is as much a challenge as it is an asset. The mind is a tool, meant to be used and put aside when not required. For a person with all three mental numbers, it is nearly impossible to put their "tool" aside. When the mental sphere dominates, it is harder to keep in regular touch with the other two aspects of existence (soul and physical planes). For example, relying on intuition is not usually a natural response for those with the Arrow of Mental Power. Often, the soul and physical planes would be considered foreign territory for them. Their home base is the mind, but the mind is also ego's playground. The mind can certainly run away with you in this instance.

To keep a healthy balance with this arrow, it is important to regularly concentrate on activities that involve the spiritual or physical aspects. Stepping down from mental sphere as much as possible will help the mind stay as a team player instead of becoming a dictator.

Keywords: Intelligent, quick-witted, humorous, creative, clever, alert, analytical, logical, attentive.

Arrow of Willpower (6, 5, 4)

	6	
	5	
	4	

This arrow's strength comes from joining the sturdiest of the base numbers—the six, five and four. These three numbers form the backbone of the birth chart. Each of these numbers are the balancers of their own plane; six keeps three and nine from going off on a tangent, five keeps two and eight from emotional imbalance, and four keeps one and seven from doing or saying the wrong thing. Despite having all three of these balancers, anyone with this arrow's combination is typically willful and pigheaded. This, in part, is due to the fact that anyone born during the last century with the Arrow of Willpower also had the Arrow of Determined Effort. Children born this century will have the benefit of experiencing the Arrow of Willpower alone, without the overshadowing of the Arrow of Determined Effort. When allowed to shine alone, the Arrow of Willpower emits strength, stability, and courage, instead of being strong-willed, forceful, and overbearing.

Rarely do people with this combination of arrows rely on their intuition or the advice of others. Often they are caught up in their own intensity and power and can't see the forest for the trees. The key to this arrow's strength lies within its ability to provide a solid energetic footing from which to branch out. Like a tree trunk is to its branches—sturdy, solid and constant. When creativity (6) joins with the freedom to express itself (5) and has the stable foundation from which to expand (4), anything is possible.

Keywords: Solid, stable, balanced, courageous, strong, forceful, willful, determined, intense, unstoppable.

Arrow of Inspiration (3, 2, 1)

3		
2		
1		

Inspired thinking sums up this arrow's energy. Linking the number of imagination (3) with the number of intuition (2) and the most isolated number (1) gives the phrase "lost in thought" a whole new meaning. Anyone with this arrow is never short on inspired ideas or plans, but they aren't always the most practical. The two's solid intuitive sense is overshadowed by the intense mental power of the three and the verbally aggressive (ego-expressive) one, making attention to the subtle details a missed step. If you happen to need an ingenious plan, look no further than someone with the Arrow of Inspiration. They'll whip you up a super-duper scheme in a jiffy— just don't count on them to hammer out the details. These people love organizing and planning to the extent that they become fanatical about it, yet they habitually forget to ensure they have their ducks in a row before executing their inspired plans. None the less, an A+ for effort must be awarded for their endless out-of-the-box thinking.

Keywords: Planner, organizer, inspired, imaginative, creative, orderly, enthusiastic, detached, impractical.

Arrow of Emotional Equilibrium (2, 5, 8)

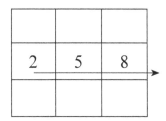

A key ingredient of intuitive sensitivity and spiritual awareness is emotional control. As humans, we aren't perfect, especially when it comes to emotions and our control over them. When using our intuition or accessing our spiritual side, nothing clouds our clear view of things quicker than out-of-control emotions. The Arrow of Emotional Equilibrium joins all three soul plane numbers, paving the way for emotional stability. Those who possess all three soul plane numbers have an inherent spiritual awareness and understanding. They are very compassionate, caring, and sensitive people, but at the same time remain detached enough so as not to get swept up in the emotional waters. Such a high level of emotional intelligence makes them superb natural counselors and healers of all kinds.

With that said, there is a downside to this number combination. The emotional and spiritual sensitivity that comes along having all three feeling numbers can be intense. Arguments or other extreme emotional situations can be taxing because there is such depth of feeling present. On a personal level, negative people, or (negative) emotionally charged situations, should be kept to a minimum.

Keywords: emotionally stable, compassionate, feeling, sensitive, intuitive, spiritually aware, loving, balanced.

ARROWS OF WEAKNESS
Defining our Challenge Areas (3 blank spaces in a row)
Whenever there are three missing numbers or blank spaces in a row on a birth chart, it highlights a main area of weakness. For example, if a chart were missing all three soul plane numbers (2, 5, 8), it would be evident that the realm of emotions and relationships would be a particularly significant challenge area for that individual.

With the Arrows of Strength, our strengths were accentuated and heightened further when any three numbers were connected in a row. Likewise, with the Arrows of Weakness, our challenge areas are also accentuated and brought to light. Although someone with an Arrow of Weakness might have larger hurdles to jump over or bigger challenges to tackle, it isn't that life has dealt them a bum deal—on the contrary. When life gives you lemons, you can make really great lemonade if you're willing to put in the effort.

Many amazing people who have had seemingly challenging lives have gone on to do great things for mankind. We are here on Earth to learn and evolve spiritually and, not surprisingly, those with the most life challenges are the ones who end up taking major leaps forward in terms of spiritual advancement and awareness. We can wallow in self-pity or we can take the bull by the horns and face our challenges head on. As a rule of thumb, the more difficult the path we have chosen to live, the greater or more significant our life purpose. Challenges build fortitude, strength of character, and bless us with humility. If you're lucky enough to have an Arrow of Weakness, consider it the mark of a warrior.

Arrow of High Expectations (missing 4, 5, 6)

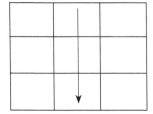

Of all the Arrows of Weakness, the Arrow of High Expectations has earned the reward for the biggest challenge area. Opposite the Arrow of Willpower, this arrow is all about unrealistic expectations. We all tend to hold expectations of how someone should act or how a situation should play out, but this arrow takes it to a whole other level. Lacking the practical four, the emotionally balanced five, and the visionary six energy, it is easy for this arrow to blow things out of proportion.

Extremely high expectations are typical when someone is missing the four, five, and six. What typically follows unrealistically high expectations is let down, disappointment, and frustration. The greatest challenge with this arrow is to learn to leave room for variance and individual differences. The vision we hold of someone or something isn't always what it turns out to be. It's difficult for someone with this arrow to shift gears and say, "Oh well, I guess that didn't work out the way I thought it would." They dwell on the disappointment of it all. "Oh woe is me" is the slogan of the Arrow of High Expectations. When we lessen our expectation of an outcome, it is less likely we will be disappointed because we leave the door open for possibilities.

Keywords: unrealistic expectations, frustration, disappointment, high ideals, uncompromising, unreasonable.

Arrow of Skepticism (missing 3, 5, 7)

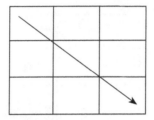

The head of this arrow is on the seven, the deep and philosophical number that is ever-searching for the deeper meaning in life. This is the basis of the Arrow of Skepticism, to uncover the truth. However, the seven is missing in this Arrow of Weakness which creates an overtone of initial distrust and questioning with anything unfamiliar. Unlike the energy of the present seven, which leaps with both feet, there is hesitancy when the seven is missing. The mentally certain three and the freely loving and expressive five are also missing in this combination. As result, uncertainty leads to cautious, protective and skeptical behavior.

Question first, trust later is the name of the game with the Arrow of Skepticism. All the facts need to be in and assessed before the verdict can be decided. These people need to feel the truth in their bones before they accept something fully and completely. Once they have found something that sits well with them, they have no trouble embracing it. Questioning the things in life is not necessarily a bad thing since doing things strictly based on blind faith can sometimes lead to trouble. The biggest obstacle with this arrow is learning to trust one's own instincts and choices. This is where the search for the meaning of life begins. Once we learn to trust ourselves, only then can we learn to trust all else.

Keywords: uncertain, skeptical, hesitant, questioning, cautious, protective, doubtful, truth-seeking.

Arrow of Emotional Sensitivity (missing 2, 5, 8)

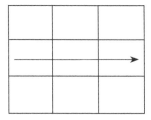

When all three soul plane numbers are present, as in the arrow of Emotional Equilibrium, the emotions find stability and intuitive and spiritual awareness are abundant. When the numbers two, five, and eight are missing, hypersensitive emotions, blocked intuition, and inner uncertainty dominates. The high degree of emotional sensitivity associated with the Arrow of Emotional Sensitivity forces walls to be built for protection, starting at an early age. In our youth, we develop coping mechanisms and protective strategies based on our experiences and carry this armor throughout life. Unfortunately, that armor can get pretty darn thick with the extreme level of emotional sensitivity that comes with this arrow.

For humans, our emotions are the most fragile of all our faculties, but for those missing all three soul plane numbers, their emotions are cripplingly fragile. When our emotions are cut off from the rest of us, our inner radar is turned off. Whether we're aware of it or not, we rely heavily on our emotions to guide us. Socially, it is very difficult to successfully interact with others without being in touch with our emotions. Intuition is something we use everyday—or at least we should be. Our emotions act as an important guidepost to help us decide if we're doing the right thing.

Hypersensitive emotions can create reactive and defensive behavior as a means of protection. Cut off emotions and defensive behavior isn't particularly great for building and keeping relationships so it no surprise to learn that the battlefield of the Arrow of Emotional Equilibrium is the realm of relationships. Despite their tendency to "lock-down" emotions, they are exceptionally loving and feeling people. The five, as the heart of this arrow, always desires to love and be loved, but the risk is often too great.

Self-esteem is how we feel about ourselves. If we feel good about the person we are, others will too. The best way to overcome the challenges presented by this arrow is to first learn to love ourselves and feel comfortable with every flaw. Find your strengths and stand tall in them. The only opinion that really matters is the one you hold of yourself.

Keywords: hypersensitive, loving, emotional, reactive, defensive, protective, indecisive, detached.

Arrow of Chaos (missing 1, 4, 7)

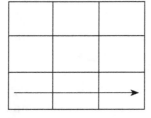

Manifesting our dreams and goals is a three-stage process of thinking, feeling, and doing. Our idea that originates in the mind is filtered through the emotions to gauge how it feels, and the last step is to take action in the physical sense. What happens if there is not enough physical energy to gain lift-off? This is exactly the case when all three physical plane numbers (1, 4, and 7) are missing.

With the Arrow of Chaos, ideas fizzle out at the doing stage; they just don't ever seem to work out as you pictured them to. Aside from that, physical motivation is not plentiful for those with this arrow. They are the thinkers and feelers, preferring to hypothesize and live in theory instead of taking action. Unfortunately, theory only takes us so far in life. At some point, to be successful in the earthly realm, we need to roll up our sleeves and get dirty.

Laziness may be a choice word for those with this arrow, but in fact, it is simply that this is their weakest link. Through no fault of their own, they're lacking a desire to physically act, and when they do take action, nothing seems easy. The best remedy for the Arrow of Chaos is to discover that physical action leads to accomplishment. There is great satisfaction (and thus motivation) in bringing an idea into tangibility. Start slowly at first, with small tasks, building bigger undertakings over time. This arrow is non-existence for anyone born in the previous century because every birth date contained at least the number one. The Arrow of Chaos will be much more common during this century as the one and nine are no longer constants in all birth dates.

Keywords: **unmotivated, apathetic, dreamer, procrastinator, underachiever, dawdler, put off.**

Arrow of Compliance (missing 7, 8, 9)

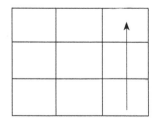

This Arrow is formed by the absence of the three most active numbers on the three planes of existence (mind, soul, physical)—the seven, eight and nine. As a result, the mental, emotional, and physical drive is lacking associated with these numbers. This Arrow, like the Arrow of Chaos, is unheard of for any birth date in the 1900s. This Arrow is becoming more common now that the nine is not a constant in all birth dates.

It would be safe to say that the word driven wouldn't be used to describe someone missing the three most active numbers. These people are the guides, the philosophers, and the peacemakers of the twenty-first century. Uninterested in achieving or climbing the corporate ladder, they're the ones who love to stop and smell the roses and this isn't a bad thing, for the most part.

Passivity isn't just about lacking drive and ambition for personal achievement, it is about a desire to live in agreement with all things rather than fighting against the current. Our spiritual essence calls for us to just be, it is our ego that drives us to accomplish and accumulate. Those with the Arrow of Compliance are ahead of the game when it comes to practicing the state of just being. They much prefer peace over war in every sense.

However, we are still spiritual beings in human form and physical action is necessary to accomplish our goals. The down side to this arrow is that physical inactivity can become a pattern to the point that not much is accomplished in the physical sense. Like the remedy for the Arrow of Chaos, consciously incorporating more physical interest and activity into daily life can work wonders, achieving a more balanced expression.

Keywords: **passive, easy-going, laid-back, calm, non-confrontational, peace-seeking**

Arrow of Postponement (missing 1, 5, 9)

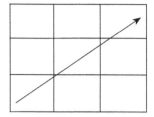

One, five, and nine form the Arrow of Determined Effort, but when these numbers are missing, procrastination dominates instead of drive and ambition. Unlike the Arrow of Determined Effort, which aggressively charges out of the gate like a pent-up bull, the Arrow of Postponement puts off or delays anything and everything. Lacking the ambitious and idealistic nine, the emotionally expressive five, and the verbal one, people with this arrow tend to look like underachievers in every sense. In truth, it isn't that they don't want to achieve, they're unsure of what they want to accomplish and how to go about doing it.

As humans, we express our mental thoughts (9) through both emotional (5) and verbal (1) means. Without those three components playing an active role in our lives, it can be a challenge to express ourselves. Similar to the Arrow of Chaos and Arrow of Compliance, practicing physical action in small steps to complete set goals and ensuring completion of a task before moving onto the next is key to successfully overcoming the problems associated with the Arrow of Postponement.

Keywords: procrastinate, put-off, stall, delay, dawdle, excuses, avoidance, discourage, dissuade.

Arrow of Limited Memory (missing 3, 6, 9)

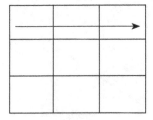

When all three Mental Plane numbers three, six, and nine are missing, the mental sphere, in particular the memory, is a challenge area. Those who possess the Arrow of Limited Memory need to consistently and constantly keep their minds active in order to maintain mental sharpness. Mental agility is not something that comes naturally as it does with the Arrow of Mental Power.

They aren't stupid or have below average intelligence. It is merely that the mental realm is not their comfort zone. Children with this arrow may seem slow in school or disinterested in schoolwork, but this should not be taken as a lack of intelligence nor should they be labeled as have attention problems. Usually, when the Arrow of Limited Memory is present, there are significant strengths on either the soul or physical planes (or both). Just because someone isn't particularly book smart doesn't mean they aren't an incredible artist or athlete. It is unfortunate that our society places so much emphasis and prestige on IQ, because the mind is really just another tool for the greater spiritual essence within us.

Although habitual lifelong mental exercise should be undertaken to keep the mind in tip-top shape, this arrow should not be considered a major handicap. It is often an indication that the individual is gifted at the soul or physical level. Many with this arrow are eccentric people. Being freed, even in small ways, from the shackles of the mind is a blessing more than it is a liability.

Keywords: absent-minded, lack of memory, forgetful, inattentive, mentally lazy, slow-learner, daydreamer.

No Arrows
Lacking Significant Strengths or Weaknesses

What does it mean when a birth chart has no arrows? The technical answer is that the person does not possess any significant strengths or weaknesses. Taken at face value, this sounds like someone who doesn't have much going for them or is rather boring. But, there is much more to be said for a lack of strong qualities than meets the eye.

Many people with strength arrows are so caught up in their own personal agendas that they aren't of much use to others along the path. Likewise, anyone with weakness arrows is regularly caught up in the drama, sacrifice, and loss that weaknesses can bring with them. Weaknesses are really significant challenges that can take up a great deal of our time and energy if we let them.

So what happens when you aren't blinded by drive and determination or you don't have huge potholes catching you up on your path? You're able to stop and smell the roses, take inventory of your surroundings, and gain a better sense of direction, which allows you to better avoid the difficult path full of challenging obstacles and potholes.

Those blessed with no arrows tend to be the happy-go-lucky type, having the time to help others since they aren't completely wrapped up in their own affairs. They're guides in their own way, because they have a knack for being able to bring us back to awareness which stops us from being blind-sided by drive or wallowing in self-pity. They can see the bigger picture as they can stop long enough to see it. Many of us can't see the forest for the trees, but someone with no Arrows can at least catch a glimpse of it from time to time.

Keywords: happy-go-lucky, content, aware, relaxed, supportive, easy-going, unassuming

Now that you know your strengths from the previous chapter, and now your weaknesses, you're prepared to start work on bringing a more balanced expression into your life and maximizing your potential for success and contentment. We need both our strengths and our weaknesses otherwise we would have no opportunity to grow and change, which is the essence of life itself. The goal is to not let one particular energy dominate, but to find a balance with all your energies or lack thereof. You don't want to be crippled by your emotional sensitivities or at the mercy of your desire to leap first and think later. To know your strengths and weaknesses is to regain your creative power over your own life. You are ultimately the creator of your own reality and knowledge is the fuel for that creation. Armed with this new information of self, you now know what mediums you have to shape your life from. It's up to you as to how you use them and what you want to create with them.

CHAPTER 7:
ARE YOU FIGHTING THE FLOW?

Recognizing & Working with the Energetic Patterns
Around You Shifts Life from Chaos to Clarity

One of the most common reasons for frustration with life is fighting the energetic flow. Since all things in life are created from energy, you're either going with the flow in the river of energy or fighting your way upstream. A good indicator of where you're at in the cycles of life is to gauge how easy your life is at this moment. The more obstacles and challenges you have, the more you're fighting the flow. In energy terms, resistance means you're trying to paddle against the current. Are you fighting the flow?

A downside to living in a world created from energy is that much of it is unseen. How do we know which way to steer our boat if we can't see the river? There are global and personal cycles of energetic patterns that we can't see, but these cycles have a great impact on the experiences and reality we create moment by moment. Knowing what these cycles are and how to work with them can be pivotal in whether or not we can successfully navigating life.

Some people seem to be more intuitively tuned in to these cycles, making their life seems easier than ours. We've all known of someone who seems to make all the right choices at all the right times and success comes easily for them. Then there are those who seem to have been dealt a bum deal in the life department with a non-stop rollercoaster of personal experience involving much sacrifice, loss, and hardship. If you're in the latter group or even somewhere in between, this next section may be the most important part of the entire book. One of first things I do for my clients is to determine what personal cycles influence them most. It can immediately explain why your extra efforts aren't yielding ample results. For example, if you attempt to make major life changes under a self-reflective or consolidative year, it's like trying to plant a garden in the winter. Life has an ebb and flow that has to be respected and appreciated.

This chapter is dedicated to helping you master the flow of life. By doing so, you'll start to see your life shift from a stormy sea to smooth sailing.

OUR JOURNEY MAPPED OUT IN NUMBERS: THE 9 YEAR CYCLES OF CHANGE

Everything in existence runs on patterns/cycles because everything is energy and energy predictably pathways of least resistance. Like the seasons, moon cycles, bodily processes, the twenty four hour clock, and many other patterns in our world, we also follow the flow of energy's predictable patterns.

The phrase "history repeats itself" is to be taken literally when talking about. Without some form of interference, energy will continue to flow toward the path of least resistance, cycling over and over again. The Mayans were way ahead of the game when they developed the calendar with its repeating cycles.

The energy patterns of all living things are affected by the other energetic patterns around them. This creates interference with the flow of energy. When energy is interrupted, it either ceases to flow or is redirected. The twenty four hour clock creates such an interruption as it forces periods of growth and rest. Much like the four seasons are brought about by the Earth's cycles, which also create periods of growth and rest.

The calendar is based on the cycles of the Earth, and our own cycles are dependent upon and in sync with the Earth's cycles. The base numbers one to nine also apply to the outer cycles that affect our lives. While the Earth's cycles change yearly (12 month calendar), our cycles are nine years in length. Within these nine year cycles, like all cycles of living things, there are periods of growth and rest.

Our birth date and the current cyclic year of the Earth determine our present year within our nine year cycle of change. Before calculating our own Personal Year we need to calculate the Earth year number.

2013 - 2+0+1+3 = 6   The Earth year number for 2013 is 6.

As everything from a numbers perspective flows in cycles of one to nine, and these are the base number patterns, one and nine form the peak of the cycle because one is the beginning and nine is the end of those cycles. Thus, most of the change we experience in life typically happens under these vibrations. In other words, our pivotal points, or major life events, usually happen during these peaks.

There is, however, one other peak in the cycle. It isn't as strong or full of change as the beginning and the end of a cycle, but is none the less a change energy. As the number of creativity and creative expression, the Personal Year of six is considered the mini peak in the cycle with its tremendous amount of creatively charged energy.

Years four and seven in the cycle are considered the rest years. These are the years when we should not attempt any major changes in our lives and should focus instead on reflection, pruning, organizing, resting, and stabilizing. Integrating and realigning ourselves after major shifts occur, we can then see where we have come and where we need to go.

One other important point is that each of the four nine year Cycles of Growth is progressively stronger in power and strength, asserting more energetic influence and potential for change and assimilation. This, of course, is a sign of our evolving development as we move along on our journey.

Let's start with discussing the Personal Year of nine as it is both the beginning of a new cycle and the end of an old.

Personal Year of 9
The Personal Year of nine is the highest change year. Its energy brings waves of change energy with it by incorporating the idealism and ambitious energy of the nine. It is a year when anything goes. People feel drawn to change jobs, locations, relationships, etc. It is also a humanitarian energy, and many feel drawn to activities that help mankind. The nine year marks both the beginning of a new cycle and the end of an old. It is a pivotal year of big change and action. If there was something you were putting off doing, a nine year is the time to do it. Some mental based people may use the high change of the nine year to mentally make their checklist of what they want to change and then take action under the following one year, which is the first physical plane number of new beginnings.

Personal Year of 1
This is the year where we absorb and integrate the changes we made while under the influence of the highest change nine year. The one energy wants us to physically adjust our lives to the changes we have made. It is a time of adjustment but can also be a time of additional

change. If you are a mental Life Theme Number, you would be more inclined to think and plan the changes you want to make under a nine influence because nine is also a mental plane number. Then, under the one energy, you would be likely to act on those plans, because one is a physical plane number. A one energy gives us more self-confidence (one is the number of verbal expression and ego expression) to adjust to our new lifestyle, and it is also a "doing" number which gives us the energy and stamina we need to get things done.

Personal Year of 2

Two is the number of intuition and sensitivity, which makes the Personal Year of two a time of inner self-reflection and spiritual growth. Heightened emotional and intuitive sensitivity is appropriately normal during a high inner growth period. Even the more active Life Theme Numbers find the energy of the two slows them down and directs them inward. Two is not a major outer change year but meant to be a year of inner soulful evolution. Greater emotional balance is also a side effect of the spiritual expansion experienced during the two year, although some find it a particularly emotionally sensitive year as well.

Flipping from such a high doing energy of the one year into the ultra quiet and peaceful two energy can be a bit too abrupt for some of the more action-packed Life Theme Numbers. This is when negativity can take hold and an emotional rollercoaster year can arise, caused by accentuated intuition and emotional sensitivity. Those who insist on continuing full force with outer change, neglecting to do any inner work, are almost certainly setting themselves up to be unsuccessful in some way. Focusing on meditation and other emotional and soulful practices is a must during a two year. The energy of the two is meant to allow us a break from all the major physical changes made during the previous two years. Life has growth and rest periods, and the Personal Year of two is most certainly a rest period to regroup and realign from the inside out.

Personal Year of 3

Three is the entry point to the mind plane, which makes the three an intellectually oriented period of growth and stimulation. The mind is usually ravenous for information and many find they read more, attend classes or courses, or feel drawn to do research in places like the internet. Some feel drawn to attend conventional forms of learning, such as going back to school, while others connect with more spiritual or personal growth. It is known as an energy that is great for writing and authors of all kinds with such an abundance of imaginative flow. There is also a desire to travel for some under a Personal Year of three for the pursuit of information. Travel may initially be booked for leisure, but it usually turns out to be an adventure filled with learning. The intelligent, perceptive, a strong memory bank, the three energy makes this particular year easier to take in and hold onto new information. Expanding and actively using the memory is important because our memory is pivotal in how we feel about ourselves and the level of self-confidence we hold.

As the social butterfly energy, the three year is isn't all about intellectual interests. Taking advantage of the social, sunny, bright and inspirational qualities of the three also makes the Personal Year of three a lot of fun too.

Personal Year of 4

As the most practical and grounded of all numbers, the Personal Year of four is a time of joining together the previous three year's energies and experiences. It's not a year where major changes should be embarked upon, but rather should be spent cleaning out the closet, both literally and figuratively, getting rid of things that no longer fit or serve us in our life. All this plucking and cleansing is meant as a means to clear the runway to make way for the upcoming freedom of expression five year. Major outer changes are not recommended and will likely be regretted if made under the influence of this year.

The four year is also meant to be a year of rest, a break in the energies to prepare for the upcoming change years. The equaling and balancing energies of the four will help to bring the body, mind, and soul back into alignment and equilibrium to prepare your essence for the rest of the nine year cycle of change.

Personal Year of 5

Five is the number of the heart and emotions representing freedom of expression. The five year is a period of personal self-expression, and the urge to express is at an all-time high under the five energy. As a career or life purpose focused year, the ability to see more clearly through the lens of the heart and soul helps us see what we truly desire, especially when it comes to our life purpose. Heart-centered expression is the theme of a five year with emotions leading the way. There is a strong draw to express your gifts, talents, and passion, because five is about living through the heart and soul. The combination of increased emotional energy and a sense of freedom to express makes the five year a time of excitement and thrill to be alive. It is absolutely the perfect time to focus on discovering your calling in life, because there is no better doorway to the soul than through the heart!

Personal Year of 6

Considered a change year (but a lesser one than the nine) in the nine year cycles, the six is all about creativity. It brings a major burst of creative juices and can be higher change energy in its own right. The mind faculties are in full tilt under a six year as the number creative expression. Any endeavors have odds of strong success when started under this year's frequency. The flip side of the six is all about relationships—starting, ending, or changing them. Many find there is a great deal of shifting within relationships on several levels. If not in a relationship, there is a desire to "nest" or settle down and find that life partner. Creating in relationships can also include adding children to the mix. As the number of extremes, it can also be a touchy year where the more negative qualities of the six, such as pessimism and perfectionism, can put a damper on the uplifting creative vibe of a six year.

Being the visionary number, it is a time to look at the bigger picture to recreate your life and revise any relationship connections to be more in alignment what you truly desire.

Personal Year of 7

Similar to the plucking, cleaning and rearranging four year, a seven year is a low outer change period. The seven year brings us inward for self-reflection. It is a time to look back at where we've gone and look ahead to what's next through reviewing and integrating the experiences of the previous six years. This is the calm before the storm and another pause year like the four to prepare for the high change years of the eight and nine, which are up next.

In addition to it being an inner change year, as the teaching learning number, the seven nudges us to share of our personal experiences as a means of learning from them. Meditation, journaling, reading, and walking in nature are all helpful tools to aid the inner work that should be the main focus during a Personal Year of seven.

Personal Year of 8

Moving out of the sober and highly self-reflective seven year, the confident and goal oriented eight year is a nice change of pace. If you've done the inner work necessary, you're ready to embrace the strong take-charge energy that the eight brings. Eight is the number of wisdom and independence, and is the most active number on the soul plane. The eight year is time to pursue your goals with gusto. Any goals or plans you might have put off are ready for lift-off this year. The extra boost of confidence, assertiveness, and doubtlessness of the eight vibration makes this high change year perfect for achievement and manifestation of all that you desire. Synchronicities are in full effect with opportunities and potential falling into your lap. Tapping into the eight's wellspring of wisdom makes this year the official no-fail year.

OUR JOURNEY MAPPED OUT IN NUMBERS: THE LARGER OUTER CYCLES OF GROWTH

The nine Personal Years we have just reviewed also fit into a larger outer cycle called the Cycles of Growth. Although we continually repeat the nine Personal Years throughout our lives, if we were on our death bed reflecting, we could divide our life up into four major chunks of time. These blocks of time don't technically begin until we enter our adult years because up until that point, we aren't mature enough to handle their energies properly.

There are four nine year Cycles of Growth and each have their own energetic overtone. These Cycles or "Peaks" run the course of twenty-seven years and mark major times of transformation and growth (both inner and outer growth). The energetic effect of each peak or cycle is frequently stronger than the previous as we gain in maturity, experience and understanding of life. As a result, we are better prepared to use the next peak's energy even better and more effectively which is why they are called the Cycles of Growth.

To calculate the age at when we begin the Cycles of Growth, subtract your Life Theme Number from the number thirty-six. Before we discuss the calculations, I would like to explain further the significance of the number thirty-six.

The number thirty-six shows up frequently in the measurements taken from analyzing the construction of the pyramids in Egypt. As well, thirty-six is the square of six and six is the number of creation. It is also the number of chapters in the fourth Book of the Bible called "Numbers."

Using the number thirty-six as the basis of the calculations of the Cycles of Growth ensures, we start each peak or cycle under the influence of the highest change year of nine. This nine year represents both the end and beginning of a new cycle. It is no coincidence that by using thirty-six we always begin a new cycle precisely at the ninth year, regardless of our Life Theme Number. This certainly shows that numerology is quite mathematical and scientific, as it is simply a means to show the flow and structure of energy. There is nothing mystical about it.

To construct our own pyramid and fill it in with the appropriate numbers, we need to first calculate numbers of the base of the pyramid. Like the calculation for the Life Theme Number, we need to reduce the three parts of the birth date to single digits.

Step 1 - The Calculation
Convert the birth date to its full numerical value. An example, Jan 14, 1978, would be 1/14/1978 (always include full year). Further reduce separately, each to a single digit, the month, day and year.

E.g. **Month** Jan (**1**) + **Day** 14(1+4=**5**)
+ **Year** 1978(1+9+7+8=25, 2+5=**7**)

Step 2 - Construction of Pyramid
The pyramid is constructed using four separate triangles. The triangles represent the spiritual mountain and our quest for truth and awareness. The pyramid is comprised of four smaller pyramids which represent the four Cycles of Growth.

Calculating 1st Peak
Using the previous example, 1/14/1978, the first Pyramid (Peak) is calculated using the Month (**1**) and Day (1+4=**5**) of the birth date. Add these two numbers to find the first Peak's numerical vibration. 1+5=6. **6** is the first Peak number. This number is placed in the "peak" of the first triangle.

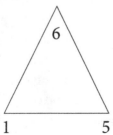

Calculating 2nd Peak

To calculate the 2nd Peak we must first draw a second triangle beside the first and place the single reduced year digit of 7 in the far right corner. Then add the Day (1+4=**5**) and the Year (1+9+7+8=25, 2+5=**7**) to find the numerical value of the 2nd Peak. 5+7=12, 1+2=**3**. The second Peak is a 3.

Note: Always reduce to single digit for 1st & 2nd Peak values.

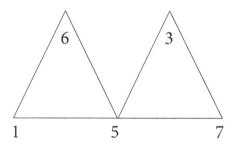

Calculating the 3rd Peak

To calculate the third peak we must first add a third triangle on top of the previous two. This creates a third triangle which will form our third peak. To calculate the value of the third peak, add the values of the first (6) and second (3) peaks. Unlike the previous two peaks, if the sum adds to a double digit we do not always reduce to a single digit. The exception is if the sum adds to 10, 11, 22/4 or 33/6. In these cases we leave the sum as is and don't reduce it. This rule only applies to the third and fourth peaks. The reason being is that these four numbers, 10, 11, 22/4 and 33/6, hold tremendous potential for growth and development as Master Numbers, but they also require an adequate level of maturity and wisdom to be properly utilized. Therefore, if these numbers appear in the first or second peaks, they are reduced to their more physical and less spiritual form (10 is 1, 11 is 2, 22/4 is 4 and 33/6 is 6). In our younger years, we often don't have an adequate level of personal experience and wisdom to properly make good use of such profound Master Number energies (which are focused on spiritual growth). We are more likely to be working on building our physical life such as succeeding in our career, buying a home, growing a family and so on.

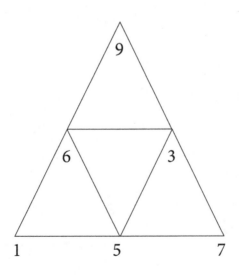

Calculating the 4th Peak

The fourth and last peak is calculated using the outer two numbers of the pyramid, the month (1) and year (7). To represent this peak we draw a fourth "open" triangle outside the pyramid structure. This triangle is missing one side and remains open to symbolize the fourth peak's energy continuing past the nine years until death.

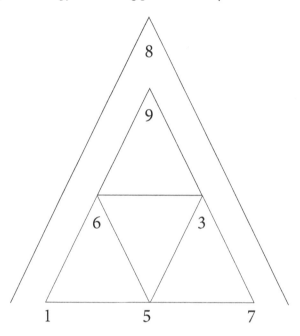

Referring again to the birth date 1/14/1978, we can now add the ages/years in which each Peak is reached. First we need to figure out the Life Theme Number of this birth date. Reduce each part of the birth date (m/d/y) to a single digit and then add together. If sum is a double digit, reduce to single digit. The birth date reduced is 1 + 5 + 7 = 13, 1+3=**4**. 4 is the Life Theme Number. Subtract 4 from 36 and you will arrive at the age in which the peaks/Cycles of Growth begin for this birth date. 36-4=**32**. Add nine years to each previous age to calculate the beginning age of each peak. For the Life Theme Number four, the ages would be 32, 41, 50, 59.

The last step of the construction process is to add the calendar year corresponding to that age. For this date of birth 1/14/1978, the year in which they were 32 was 2010 (1978 +32= 2010). Add nine years to each of the previous calendar dates to fill in the remaining dates. The calendar years for this birth date are 2010, 2019, 2028, 2037.

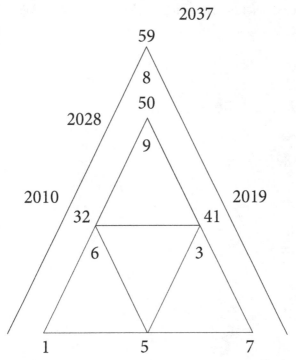

Now we're ready to analyze it!

Step 3 - Analyzing the Data

The pyramid structure we just created holds within it the map of your path. We have discussed who the *real* you is, and now it is time to find out where this real you is going in this life. The peaks are periods of growth and development and each peak's numerical vibration can give us clues as to what we will be doing during those years in our lives. Whether it is a physical "doing" number or a spiritual, reflective number, knowing what that energy is can help us go with the flow instead of trying to fight our way upstream. For example, if we try to make changes under a very reflective time, we are most certainly setting ourselves up for failure.

The next section contains the meanings of the eleven possible peak cycles we may be under the influence of at some point in our life. Not every peak cycle is meant for you, and only four of them (or less if there are multiples of the same cycle energy) will be yours. If you were on your death bed at let's say the ripe age of 100, you could reflect back and divide your life into four main chunks of time. Some people refer to parts of their life thus far as being another lifetime in many respects. This is because the energy shifts gears at such a fast pace, it seems like a new life altogether. This happens every nine years starting from at predetermined age starting sometime in your twenties or thirties, depending on your Life Theme number. Until that point in life, we are still in the growth phase of childhood, not yet ready to embark on our path and purpose.

Just as the birth chart maps out our inner self, the peak cycles map out our outer journey and how we can best use our inherent tools, trait, strengths, and weaknesses for soulful growth and development through personal experience and contemplation. Like all cycles, keep in mind that there will always be times of growth and times of rest. Recognizing when you need to rest or when it's time to take action can make the difference between a life that is smooth sailing or one full of brick walls.

Peak of 1

Expressing yourself through doing is the theme of this peak. As one is the first number on the physical plane, it is physical-based and is also the number of verbal and ego expression. It is the second highest change year and is often used as a time to adjust and tweak the tornado of changes that happened under the highest change nine year (nine and one form the top of the nine year change cycle). As the stand-alone isolated number, any underlying issues will be dug up and brought out into the spotlight to be dealt with. Aggressive and achievement oriented, the Personal Year of one is a put your nose-to-the-grindstone kind of energy. In youth, a period of one is the time to establish career, get married, build a house, and start a family. Carrying the essence of the pioneer and trailblazer, it is a time to build your empire and leave your mark on the world.

Peak of 2

Two is the number of intuition and sensitivity, and so this peak is all about inner self-analysis. It is not a period of change or growth in the physical sense but almost exclusively a period of inner growth and spiritual advancement. A focus on spiritual living in all areas is the theme of the peak of two. Emotions will be extra touchy and sensitive during a peak of two.

Depending on the current level of maturity achieved, a two cycle can turn out to be a period of intense spiritual evolution and intuitive advancement, or it can create emotions to run high and excess sensitivity to build. A peak of two is for our emotional/spiritual development and not meant for physical achievement or accumulation.

Peak of 3

As the gateway number to the mind plane, mental faculties are the main emphasis during a peak of three. Being a time for learning, analyzing, and reviewing, some lean toward traditional learning while others are drawn to learn in more unconventional ways. Travel for the purpose of continued mind growth is a popular avenue of learning during a three energy. As the social butterfly energy, the three is up for a good time too and learning doesn't have to be boring. If there are no pathways to stimulate the mindful part of self and fulfill the desire to accumulate knowledge, the three becomes critical, whiny, and demanding.

Peak of 4

The four energy is all about physical and materialistic achievement. As the number of practicality and the middle physical plane number, it is very much a doing period. If you're willing to put in the hard work and effort, much success can be accomplished under a peak of four. No new projects should be started under a four energy, but whatever you already have on-going will benefit from the high doing nature of the four. As a period of pruning, sorting, and cleaning out the closets of life, the four's practical basis cleans house, getting rid of what no longer serves the highest good. Both the four and seven are major energies where outer change is not encouraged, as it is meant to be a period of regrouping and reorganizing your life. In addition to the strong foundational repairing and building done under this frequency, it is also imperative to allow time for some rest and play to keep at bay the four's tendency toward being too focused on physical achievement.

Peak of 5

Five is the number of the heart and emotions, so the main theme of a peak of five is the seeing clearly through the lens of the heart to discover what the soul wants to express. The heart doesn't doubt, and so there is a stronger sense of the emotional self during this cycle. A side effect of emotional clarity is intuitive strength and the ability to see clearly what the heart wants. From this greater viewpoint many find their life purpose or passion under a peak of five. I was under a Personal Year of five and a peak cycle of five when I left the corporate world to embark on the more spiritual path. Most feel called to change or shift their career path in some way, as they realize they aren't on the right path (which is what happened to me).

Peak of 6

With six being the number of creativity and creative expression, this peak is meant to be focused on intense creative expression. The creative power of the Peak of six is often honed in on family and relationships. Some find that the six energy draws them to want to "nest" when those not in a relationship desire to settle down and start a family. If already married, the focus is geared toward the home and the relationships they contain. If the creative power of the six is only used in the realm of relationships, the negative qualities of the six emerge. There isn't much positive creating happening, which is the key to the six energy remaining balanced and moving forward. As the number of extremes, stagnant creative energy forces the six into a downward negative spiral. Making a point to actively create outside the arena of relationships and the home life is essential in fully utilizing the creative power of six.

Peak of 7

Cycles four and seven are the main periods when we take a rest on the spiritual mountain and regroup. It is a time to reflect and readjust our lives on many levels. A seven peak is not meant for outer change but better used to go within to re-examine, looking back to where we've gone and looking ahead to where we want to go. Seven is the teaching/learning number as well as the most active number on the physical plane, which means it learns best through personal experience. It is also a time to share wisdom through telling of lessons learned. There is no better way to learn than through personal experience, and for the seven energy, it integrates information from lessons experienced more easily when they are able to share what they know with others.

Combinations of the seven energy are greater inner change catalysts than others. Some of our most memorable experiences are those which involve a certain degree of sacrifice, loss and/or hardship. This can aid greatly in our soul's evolution. Most come out of a cycle of seven feeling like they are a different person than when they started.

Peak of 8

The eight is wise, assertive, and independent, and so the theme of a peak of eight is active independence. Many feel a boost of self-confident and self-esteem under an eight energy because the eight is doubtless as the direct link to the spiritual realm. As a house energy, the eight can be called the "divorce" house because the assertive nature can bring up issues that might have been swept under the rug. This is similar for the peak of eight where relationships will be put into the spotlight, and the partner holding the eight frequency will no longer tolerate the relationship issues.

The peak of eight is a perfect time to go after your goals in a big way, but the optimum path to take depends on your Life Theme Number. If the Life Theme Number is even, financial success is the focal point. If an uneven Life Theme Number, artistic or academic endeavors are usually the aim. Under a cycle of eight, be careful when choosing who you spend time with. They could dampen or hinder the confident and go-getter energy of the peak of eight.

Peak of 9

As the idealistic and justice-seeking humanitarian number, there is a strong desire to be of service to fellow man during a peak of nine. As with any guiding frequency, others are subconsciously attracted to the nine's helping vibe. Nine creates the ideal conditions to be of service, it can be a demanding time. Nine, being the highest change number, it is also a time when you feel the need to reinvent the wheel. Jobs, locations and relationships are some of the changes topping the list under a peak of nine.

As the most active mental plane number, some people may use this time to make changes and move forward. It is fair to say that most people will experience outer change during the nine peak season.

Peak of 10

Ten is the Earth Guide energy, and those under the influence of a peak of ten will feel the need to share their wisdom for the purpose of guiding others. It may take the form of mentoring, teaching, or counseling, but most people will feel the tug of this powerful frequency.

A peak of ten can only occur during the third and fourth peak cycles, and when it appears during the first two, it is reduced to its more physical form of one. This reason is due to the fact that children and young adults aren't equipped to handle the guiding nature of the ten. It can be a very satisfying period in life where all your experiences and knowledge are put to good use, and you enjoy the fruits of your labor. Others will subconsciously feel the guiding force of the ten and be automatically drawn to you for advice and counsel. As the old saying goes, "When the student is ready, the teacher appears."

Peak of 11
Similar to the peak of ten, a peak of eleven is only possible during the last two cycles of the four Cycles of Growth. If an eleven shows up during the lower half of the cycles, it is reduced to the more subdued two energy since during our younger years, we don't have the maturity and wisdom to fully utilize the power of the spiritual eleven. Like the ten, the eleven requires a great deal of life experience to facilitate the maturation process in order to properly utilize the highest spiritual number. On a personal level, the eleven is meant for spiritual expansion. As the base pattern, the reduced version of the eleven is an intuitive and sensitive two as the base pattern. One way that the eleven energy urges us to guide is to lead by showing. More powerfully spiritual than just the two alone, the eleven brings with it such intense spiritual energy that our own inner work and reflection will bring inspire others.

FIGHT OR FLOW

Since we are souls in human physical form, it is important for us to be aware of the cycles and patterns of energy that makes up the world around us. If all things are energy, we are constantly exposed to many other energetic frequencies that permeate and change the flow of our own energy. Energy remains free-flowing and in motion until it encounters resistance. How we allow the outer energies of the outside world to interact with our own essence plays a part in the shaping of the trajectory of our life. We can choose to fight against the current, creating more resistance than necessary, or we can go with the flow. The choice is all ours.

CHAPTER 8:
THE MASK YOU SHOW THE WORLD
Your Name Represents the Energy of Your Personality (Ego Expression)

Contrary to popular belief, our name isn't something our parents stuck on us at birth, and is some curse we must live with. A name, like our date of birth, is a pre-chosen part of our destiny before we incarnate. In my practice, I have yet to find someone whose name is not perfectly suited to who they are. Names are certainly not haphazard and serve a big purpose in how others perceive us.

As we have learned, our birth date reveals to us our spiritual DNA, and the inner workings of who we are on a soul level. Our name, on the other hand, represents the "mask" we show the world. On first meeting, not everyone sees that you may be emotionally sensitive, but they do feel the persona that is shown through the energy of your name. How does the world see you?

When I was pregnant with my daughter, I fretted for the entire nine months over name choices. Her tag on the hospital bassinette read "Baby Arbeau," and on day three, the nurse came in with the dreaded name registration papers. To this day, I chuckle when I think back to that time and the tremendous amount of effort I put into searching for a perfect name. In hindsight, I realize that the name I ended up choosing was perfect for her. It was one of the first names I had on my initial list; the one I was drawn to over and over again. Are names chosen by chance or are they also a pre-determined part of our energetic makeup? I absolutely believe the latter is true.

When I got married, I had a hard time accepting my husband's last name. I wanted to create the traditional family unit for my daughter by all of us sharing a surname. At the same time, I was fearful of losing my identity, the person I was for so many years prior. I think many women struggle with this issue, but little did I know there was a much bigger identity crisis tied up in that name change. I ended up changing my name on the day we got hitched at the Justice of the Peace. I was a rebellious gal back then, and a traditional wedding wasn't my thing. I was six months pregnant and an emotional wreck. I cried for the loss of my identity in private, but it was done, and I had to live with my choice.

Fast-forward a year later, and the real reason for the name change came into full view. My daughter was very young when I learned about the numbers and numerology. While she was napping one day, I remember calculating my maiden name as well as my new married name. It was an aha moment indeed. My new name combination was a seven, the teaching learning number of truth. It represented my new career path as a numerologist, truth-seeker, and truth-revealer, which is precisely what I now do as a career. I had always been a practical truth-seeker and was often referred to in my corporate days as "Tell it like it is Michelle." I just couldn't stand anything that wasn't the truth.

The point of the story is that my new name combination, the one I was so reluctant to accept, represented the real me; the one I embrace wholeheartedly. I see this so often with clients. As they step onto their path and purpose, they spontaneously have a strong desire to revert back to their maiden name, tweak the spelling of their first name, or go by initials. The majority of the time, the new intuitively decided upon name perfectly reflects who they are transforming into.

A name can shape our experience with others. First impressions are more than just visual. We feel energy when we meet someone or when we read their name somewhere. Have you ever heard someone call out the wrong name and apologize claiming you look just like their friend? This happens because we are subconsciously reading the energy of those we meet. We're picking up unseen energetic cues that we're interpreting. Your name is one of the first energies others encounter when they meet you. What exactly is it saying to them? Let's find out.

NAME NUMBER

The Name Number can complement, strengthen, or oppose the energy of your main essence (Life Theme Number). If the base energy of your name is the same as the Life Theme Number, it is a "what you see is what you get" scenario where the name strengthens your energy. When they are different, but from the same plane of existence (soul based Life Theme Number with a soul based name), it can bring balance. For example, if you are a sensitive and intuitive two but you have a confident, assertive and independent eight name, it can help to fill in energies you may be lacking in your date of birth.

The most preferred names are the ones that contrast the Life Theme Number. In this way, it diversifies your overall energetic makeup, allowing for the widest range of energies.

Birth charts that are full of missing spaces may benefit from a strong, expressive name. Remember, our name is our personality expression, which is our first line of interaction with others. It should compliment what we need to accomplish in terms of our life lessons (attract the right people, places, things to facilitate the experiences necessary) as well as what we desire to create in life.

Our first name holds the most energetic influence. If you use a nick name, this is the energy you want to explore first. Our first name is the name that resonates with everyone since we use it on a daily basis. Calculating the meaning of the middle and last name is less important but still has its place, as you'll see in the next section.

The full name is the underlying representation of our personality. Regardless of the hats we might wear, our full name vibration is always there as an undercurrent.

Our professional name (first and last) is important in formal situations, like career or financial matters, where papers are signed. When we hand someone a business card, what energy are they picking up from our professional name?

Calculating of the Name Number is the same as calculating the Life Theme with one additional step. The first step is to assign numerical meaning to each letter in our name (please see chart below).

NAME CONVERSION CHART

1	2	3	4	5	6	7	8	9
A	B	C	D	E	F	G	H	I
J	K	L	M	N	O	P	Q	R
S	T	U	V	W	X	Y	Z	

Using the name Michelle as an example, this is how the Complete Name Number is calculated:

M	I	C	H	E	L	L	E
4	9	3	8	5	3	3	5

Add the numbers together and reduce the number to a single digit.

$$4+9+3+8+5+3+3+5=40 \quad 4+0=4$$

The name MICHELLE adds to a 4.

FULL BIRTH NAME:
Your full birth name is like an underlying stamp or tattoo you receive at birth that represents your truest personality. Regardless of the various hats or masks you might wear in different social situations. Most of us don't use our birth name in day-to-day life, but this name still remains our truest representation of our personality throughout life.

PROFESSIONAL NAME:
Your professional name is the vibration you send out in your professional life. It is comprised (usually) of your first and last name. Is your name's vibration attracting clients/customers, or is it sending them away? Often times name changes, like in marriage or switching to a nickname/abbreviation (e.g. J.K. Rowling) can assist you in your career. When you hand someone a business card, you want your name's vibration to resonate with them.

FIRST NAME/NICKNAME/ABBREVIATIONS:
Your first name is the name that is spoken the most, and it represents your day-to-day mask. It is the name that most people associate with. When someone at work mentions your name or your friend develops a pet name for you, what does that say about you? How do people feel when they speak your first name? The frequency could be holding you back. Analyzing it is important to reveal any

blockages that might be present in the combination used most by you and everyone else. Your first name can be complimentary to your main essence or a black and white contrast. Both might be beneficial, depending on what energies you need to achieve balance. If you have a more subdued Life Theme Number (like the two or four) and work in sales, a strong first name (like a confident eight energy) would work best for you.

From my experience, most people aren't keen on changing their name, even if they don't like it. However, we can still play with the combinations such as adding a middle initial on a business card, to come up with a frequency you feel good about.

NAME NUMBER MEANINGS 1-9

Below are the nine base Name Number Meanings from one to nine. If you get a Master Number frequency (10, 11, 22, 33) leave it as it is. Although the base number is the true name vibration, it is important to note that it also carries the frequency of a Master Number. This indicates that this name is meant to be seen as a guide, and the person's life path will likely reflect that. After all, nothing in life is coincidental, including names.

The keywords after each number are repeats of the keyword definitions you saw back in chapter three. A number generally has the same overall meaning wherever you see it, with slight variations depending on how is it used. Simply put, this means these keywords apply to all vibrational energy.

Name Number 1

Those wearing the mask of the one have the Earth Guide energy of the ten, but, are living through trailblazing and ego-centered physically based one. With no balance of the softer zero, as the symbol of the infinite and spiritual awareness, others see the one mask as the go-getters, over-achievers, and sometimes overly aggressive. If your name's vibrational energy is a one, be aware that it is the most forceful energy. This can isolate you from those around you.

Keywords: **Verbal self-expression, initiate, action, ambitious, determined, pioneering, aggressive, egocentric, over-driven.**

Name Number 2
The only name that reduces to the two frequency is the one that adds to twenty first. The pure two is an extremely gentle supporting energy (as it combines the energies of the two, the number of intuition and sensitivity) with the zero (symbol of the infinite or spiritual awareness). From my experience, behind every great leader is a two. Basically, this means that the two carries a gentle and supportive guiding energy. Those who wear this mask as a name display themselves as more of a "behind the scenes" guiding force.

Keywords: **contrast, balance, cooperation, sensitive, intuitive, supportive, co-dependent, uncertain, submissive, passive.**

Name Number 3
As the intellectual, imaginative, and inspirational number, the person wears the mask of inspirationalist. The social butterfly three can light up any room and be the life of the party. When wearing this mask, others sense you are able to connect their dots and help them become complete (three is also the number of unity). It can also be used as a means to hide by putting on a "happy face" even when you don't feel that way inside. The world sees you as the bright light that attracts others to them like a moth to a flame.

Keywords: **analytical, intelligent, humorous, social, sensitive, observant, critical, vain, grandeur, self-doubting.**

Name Number 4
Four is the number of practicality and organization, making it a very grounded and physically-based energy. You wear the mask of the very approachable and trustworthy leader. People are not intimidated but rather comforted in your down-to-earth vibe. In many social or

team situations, the four is the go-to person for decision making. People often will bounce ideas off of them, as they usually have the most realistic outlook.

Keywords: endurance, progress, foundation, practical, organization, solid, stable, materialistic, impatient.

Name Number 5

The five mask is one of love, freedom of expression, compassion, and truth. It is the most free to express of all masks, but it is also one of the most sensitive. Fives are full of empathetic energy. As the number of compassion and love, it makes a perfect mask for those meant to take on the role of counselor, teacher, spiritual guide, mentor, etc. Others literally feel the love radiating from those wearing this mask. It can also take on some of the more negative qualities of the five by displaying freedom seeking, rebellion, and control.

Keyword: loving, sensitive, irregular, artistic, freedom-seeking, passionate, uncertain, power-hungry, dominating, bossy, withdrawn, moody.

Name Number 6

As the number of creativity, this is the "mother" mask, or the "creative nurturer." People come to you as a shoulder to lean on and seek solace in your warmth. Using this name, you wear the mask of mother or nurturer in relationships. Sixes also are creative visionaries who connect the dots for others. Sometimes, in the negative, it can sway toward being gossipy, critical, and pessimistic.

Keywords: creative, responsible, nurturing, home-loving, peace-maker, doting, worry-wart, people-pleaser, hostess, gossipy, pessimistic.

Name Number 7

Seven is the teaching/learning number, the truth seeker, and the deep, philosophical number. Wearing this mask, people intuitively sense you have the answers for them.

This name sometimes adds to the same vibration as the word hate (16/7), which resonates to a volatile energetic vibration. The 16/7 is an energy of rapid learning through personal experience involving sacrifice, loss, or hardship. It "strips us clean," preparing us for a new beginning. Whenever a seven is worn as a mask, it indicates the person is a truth seeker; they are the questioners and they seek answers with a deeper meaning.

There is no better form of learning than through personal experience. Early life is set up to facilitate personal experience (involving sacrifice, loss, etc.). This is a way to accumulate wisdom and knowledge for your life's purpose. The hardships you've endured, especially in the arena of relationships, have given you a wealth of wisdom from which to drawn upon as you prepare to embrace you role as guide and teacher.

Keywords: **wise, contemplative, achiever, truth-seeker, determined, stubborn, active, distrustful, hesitant.**

Name Number 8
Eight is the number of wisdom and independence. It is the wise sage energy. Wearing this mask, you come across as the knowledge-bearer. People instinctively go to you for advice or your opinion. It is a confident, assertive energy that allows you to stand taller and more assured in your personal power. This is especially true when the birth chart, or Life Theme Number, contain more subdued and sensitive energies. The eight name demands respect and usually gets it.

Keywords: independent, wise leader, loving, assertive, confident, dynamic, detached, selfish, cold.

Name Number 9
As the idealistic humanitarian, those with this name vibration present themselves as leaders for the people. They are justice-seekers

who are kind and giving. People are drawn to them because they sense leadership energy. Others recognize a nine is on their side. In the negative, the black-and-white or right-and-wrong thinking can shine through, especially if the Life Theme Number is mental based, or there is an abundance of mental energy on the birth chart. This makes the nine mask judgmental, opinionated, and generally pessimistic.

Keywords: humanitarian, ambitious, responsible, justice-seeking, idealistic, unselfish, driven, opinionated, judgmental.

Name Number 10
Wearing the mask of the Earth Guide number ten guides through casual conversation rather than preaching from the mountain-top. People intuitively sense you have grounded, wise energy, and they are drawn to it for advice or counsel. You will lead the people from a very involved standpoint as the ten combines the energies of the pioneering one with the soulful symbol of the infinite (0).

Keywords (1): Verbal self-expression, initiate, action, ambitious, determined, pioneering, aggressive, egocentric, over-driven.

Keywords (0): infinite, expansive, awareness, spiritual, neutral, open

Name Number 11
As a mask, the eleven shows itself as the cooperative and gentle guide. It is even gentler than the humanitarian nine mask, and is dubbed the "Spiritual Guide." The eleven is comprised of the pioneering/verbally expressive double one energy, and it reduces to the intuitive/sensitive/cooperative two energy. With the added spiritual element, it is still a highly active doing energy, but a more supportive and peaceful action energy. When you wear this mask, people sense you only want what was is best for them.

Keywords (1): Verbal self-expression, initiate, action, ambitious, determined, pioneering, aggressive, egocentric, over-driven.

Keywords (2): contrast, balance, cooperation, sensitive, intuitive, supportive, co-dependent, uncertain, submissive, passive.

Name Number 22/4

The twenty-two-four is one of the Master Number frequencies, which are the special energies that carry a greater responsibility. This particular number is the "Master Builder." In addition to carrying all the qualities of the four, because it has double twos (the number of intuition and sensitivity), it provides a strong spiritual component within the grounded force of the four. This makes the twenty-two-four energy a balanced gentle guide that is not afraid to get in the trenches with the people.

Keywords (4): endurance, progress, foundation, practical, organization, solid, stable, materialistic, impatient.

Keywords (2): contrast, balance, cooperation, sensitive, intuitive, supportive, co-dependent, uncertain, submissive, passive.

Name Number 33/6

This is the mother mask, the creative nurturer but with a greater guiding role. Those around you see you as a shoulder to lean on and seek out your inviting counsel. Using this name, you wear the mask of "mother" or "nurturer" in relationships as well as the creative visionary who brings the bigger picture into view. In addition, this particular combination of the six is the Master Teacher Number. The master frequencies not only hold a greater responsibility to mankind, but they have a bigger vision, path, and purpose than other energies. Wearing the mask of the Master Teacher emphasizes your mission to share truth.

Keywords (6): creative, responsible, nurturing, home-loving, peace-maker, doting, worry-wart, people-pleaser, hostess, gossipy, pessimistic.

Keywords (3): analytical, intelligent, humorous, social, sensitive, observant, critical, vain, grandeur, self-doubting.

CHAPTER 9: YOUR SOULFUL EXPRESSION: PAST, PRESENT, FUTURE

Karmic Numbers, Heart's Desire
and How You Express Your Gift to the World

Your soul is a continuous energetic pattern that never ceases to exist, unlike the physical body, which grows old and perishes. It, therefore, carries energies from previous lives and is shaped by them to form new lives to fulfill the lessons yet to be learned.

Reincarnation is thought to be the survival of the soul or spirit beyond physical death and continuing on to once again come back to Earth to live out another lifetime in a physical body. There have been some remarkably credible studies done on the theory of incarnation by the late Dr. Ian Stevenson. Dr. Stevenson has devoted the last forty years to the scientific documentation of past life memories of children from all over the world. He has over 3000 cases in his files. Many people, including skeptics and scholars, agree that these cases offer the best evidence yet for reincarnation.[11]

This chapter represents the past, present, and future of your soul's expression and how you can best utilize those energies for maximum success in all areas of your current lifetime and beyond.

Past: Karmic Lesson Numbers

The Karmic Lesson Numbers represent the energies we may be carrying forward from other lifetimes. Although we have our current lesson plan laid out in this lifetime, there may be additional lessons added to our plate that we didn't finish up from other lives.

The Karmic Lesson Numbers are derived from our full birth name. Use the Name Conversion Chart below to assign numerical values to your entire birth name. This time, you don't need to find the sum of the name but rather look to see which numbers from one to nine the full birth name is missing (see the name example below).

NAME CONVERSION CHART

1	2	3	4	5	6	7	8	9
A	B	C	D	E	F	G	H	I
J	K	L	M	N	O	P	Q	R
S	T	U	V	W	X	Y	Z	

B	E	T	H
2	5	2	8

L	E	A
3	5	1

A	M	B	R	O	S	E
1	4	2	9	6	1	5

In this example, let's see how many numbers are present in order to discover what numbers are missing:

1. Three Ones

2. Three Twos

3. One Three

4. One Four

5. Three Fives

6. One Six

7. Zero Sevens

8. One Eight

9. One Nine

This name has just one Karmic Lesson Number (missing numbers in the name) - the seven. Let's find out what it means to be missing the frequency of seven in our name or any of the other nine Karmic Lesson Numbers.

Here are the nine Karmic Lesson Numbers and their meanings:

KARMIC LESSON NUMBER 1

One is the pioneer number and the number of new beginnings. It is the first Physical Plane number and is high on action, risk-taking, and taking action in general. However, as a Karmic Number, learning how and when to take action is the very lesson itself, so there is often hesitancy with taking a leap forward. Often Karmic one's need coaxing before they can take a step forward. There is a need to understand and fully integrate the truth that, without action, we cannot create in life. Many without the one energy in their name tend to feel ungrounded.

Karmic Lesson Number 2

The main lesson with this Karmic Number is a need to learn patience, cooperation, and attention to detail. Relying on intuition, or the more sensitive aspects of the self, is not automatic and needs to be developed. Balance and harmony in all aspects of life can be achieved by learning the lessons associated with the Karmic Lesson Number two. Two is the number that most closely resonates with our spiritual self and is the number of intuition, sensitivity and cooperation.

Karmic Lesson Number 3
Three is the gateway number to the Mind Plane and is the number of imagination and memory. Social expression and mental alertness are the areas of focus or development. Expression of the self is the highlighted area of development here. Scattered thoughts and unclear mental focus combined with uncontrolled emotions are the greatest hurdles.

Karmic Lesson Number 4
The main lesson with the Karmic Number four is building a foundation in life. Four is the solid, practical and loyal number that is the same frequency used by the spiritual realm to manifest into the physical. There is a need for grounding and stability more on a soulful level to feel stable and safe in your being with this Karmic Number.

Karmic Lesson Number 5
Five is the number of the heart/emotions, and it represents freedom of expression. Missing this energy in your birth name says you may not be the most emotionally expressive. Too, work is usually needed to more openly express your inner self and/or emotional self.

Karmic Lesson Number 6
Six is the creative, nurturing, and a visionary energy. The main lesson with the Karmic Number six is the need to learn responsibility as well as develop dedication toward the service of others. Karmic sixes have trouble seeing the bigger picture, and they rarely comprehend that their actions have a ripple effect amongst their closest connections.

Karmic Lesson Number 7
Seven is the truth-seeker number and the teaching/learning number. Hindsight learning and personal experience involving sacrifice

and loss are how the seven energy learns. The main lesson with the Karmic Number seven is developing self-trust and trusting others. It highlights a need to work on trusting yourself first by relying on your intuition more. As result of gaining a stronger sense of inner self trust is the ability to trust others as well.

Karmic Lesson Number 8

As the number of wisdom and independence, the Karmic Number eight brings issues with confidence, assertiveness, and independence —particularly when centered on money, power, and fame. In leadership roles, especially managerial or professional roles, there is an undercurrent of feelings of insecurity, which is the opposite of the naturally confident eight. To develop what is lacking with the Karmic Number eight, practice stepping into your power, knowing you are capable and strong.

Karmic Lesson Number 9

The main lesson with the Karmic Number nine is the need to develop compassion, tolerance, and understanding of others. As the nine is the humanitarian number, you need to learn to do things for the greater good instead of personal gain. The tendency with this karmic number is to use the ambition and idealism for egocentric reasons, failing to realize the purpose of the nine energy, which is to use wisdom and integrity to help mankind.

Present: Heart's Desire Number - What is Your Soul Most Yearning to Express?

Although your Life Theme Number can show you what your main essence and what your life path or purpose is, the Heart's Desire Number can define your unique expression or gift to the world. This is one of the main reasons why you might have, for example, two Life Theme Number sevens, but they can be quite different in terms of what they want to do in life. The Heart's Desire Number represents the sparkle or fire beneath the main essence.

Some people live more through their Heart's Desire Number than their Life Theme Number. While that is not usually advisable, if it is a stronger vibration than their Life Theme Number, it can become their underlying driving force.

The Heart's Desire definitions that follow this section are an overview of how to best fine-tune your path and purpose. It doesn't, however, go into the more negative aspects of the base numbers one to nine. It is important to remember that when analyzing the Heart's Desire Number there is a positive and negative side to every base number from one to nine, whether it is a Life Theme Number, Name Number, Heart's Desire Number or any other form. It can be beneficial to explore both sides of that number as it may be that you aren't utilizing it as best as you could be. Recognizing that you might be living negatively will help you to shift gears and make the necessary changes. If you don't resonate with the qualities of your Heart's Desire Number, go back to the main base number definitions in chapter three to see if you are leaning into the negative traits of the number.

Also, if the Heart's Desire Number adds to a Master Number 10, 11, 22, or 33, write it out in its truest form (e.g. 11/2) and review these special meaning definitions in the previous chapter. Make note that a Master Number has a spiritual guiding essence associated with it, and it carries a greater responsibility in terms of how life purpose affects others.

The Heart's Desire Number is found by adding your month and day of birth together and reducing it to a single digit. Let's look at an example:

(Month) 5 (Day) 26

5+2+6=13

Reduce it further to get the base number from 1-9:

1+3=**4**

The Heart's Desire Number for this month/day example is 4.

Below are the definitions for the nine Heart's Desire energies.

Heart's Desire Number 1
Whether it's a ten or a one at the base, this Heart's Desire Number is the pioneer energy with an emphasis on verbal self-expression. If you've got this number as your Heart's Desire, you want to verbally express yourself from a soul level. As the gateway number to the Physical Plane, you aren't going to sit around and wait for things to happen, you're going to go make it happen and speak your mind to help get it done.

Heart's Desire Number 2
The Heart's Desire Number two has a focus of support. You desire to bring harmony and balance to those you are assisting. It is the peaceful, harmonious, and cooperative number, and it is a natural counselor/guiding energy. It is the same frequency that dominates the twenty-first century. Many of the children born today intuitively resonate with those who carry a Heart's Desire Number two.

Heart's Desire Number 3
You are the inspirationalist in all you aspire to accomplish. You are happiest when you are uplifting and inspiring others, showing them how beautiful they are. It is a sunny, bright energy that only aims to inspire. A minor side to this number is the intellectual energy it carries. The knowledge seeker wars with the purpose to inspire others.

Heart's Desire Number 4
Practicality is the key trait of the Heart's Desire Number four. You approach everything from a grounded and solid perspective, including your spirituality. It is about merging the spiritual with the physical. Four is the same frequency that the spiritual realm uses to permeate the physical. Fours manifest themselves in solid form, so this number often is referred to as the Earth Angel energy.

Heart's Desire Number 5
Heart-centered and compassionate is the focus of the Heart's Desire Number five. You care deeply and only want to spread the love. It is also strongly about freedom of expression, and many who carry this number forge their own path and don't care for the nine-to-five grind. Anything you focus on has to be for the greater good and make people feel fantastic since anyone with the Heart's Desire Number give operates on how it makes them feel.

Heart's Desire Number 6
You are the nurturer, the motherly visionary who can connect the dots for other people. You can naturally see the bigger picture and tend to be the go-to person. Whatever your Life Theme Number energy, you are meant to bring it all together for others and help them become whole and complete.

Heart's Desire Number 7
As the truth-seeker number and a natural scientist's outlook, you are always seeking the deeper meaning in everything. You search for truth through your actions as a means to help others do the same. You lead by example, as seven is the most active "doing" number on the Physical Plane. Most people who carry this Heart's Desire Number attract an abundance of personal experience. This facilitates their ability to seek and reveal truth, not only for themselves but for others.

Heart's Desire Number 8
As the number of wisdom and independence, the Heart's Desire Number eight is all about the spreading wisdom and knowledge. This doesn't mean those who have this Heart's Desire Number will quit their day job and join a monastery, but they do seem to have both an ability to say the right thing at the right time. Eight has a direct link to the spiritual realm, and so words of wisdom seem to flow easily. They are essentially here to spread wisdom and knowledge in many forms and pathways.

Heart's Desire Number 9

The humanitarian number nine creates a Heart's Desire Number that consistently wants to help mankind in all they do. In the positive, it is a very selfless and justice-seeking energy—always for the people. Those with this Heart's Desire Number aren't short on opinion, and they gravitate toward a career or role that allows them to speak for the people. They are only content when helping others change for the better.

FUTURE: HOW WILL YOU SHARE YOUR GIFT WITH THE WORLD?

The sum of your year of birth shows you the pathway through which you will share all of your energies, particularly how you express your Life Theme Number and Heart's Desire Number patterns.

To calculate this number frequency, add each individual digit in your date of birth and, as always, reduce to a single digit to find the base pattern. Here is an example:

$$1+9+7+8=25$$

$$2+5=7$$

This is my own year of birth, and it reduces to the seven, the teaching/learning truth-seeker number, as well as the most active physical plane number. My expression pathway is definitely the teacher and the truth seeker/revealer, which is what I do for others in my work. I prefer to show rather than preach, which is typical of the very physical seven pattern and its rebellious lead-by-example style.

This is the final piece of the puzzle to complete the total energetic expression of self. This calculation answers how you prefer to express your energies outwardly. There are no specific definitions for this particular calculation, so after you've calculated which number your expression pathway is, refer to the base number meanings from one to nine below for your number definition.

The Base Number Meanings (One to Nine and Zero)

1 One is the first physical plane number. It governs our communications skills and verbal self-expression through the ego. One is the only complete number, representing our divine expression through the physical. As the number most linked to ego, it is a driven and active energy, seeking achievement and success. **Keywords: verbal self-expression, initiate, action, ambitious, determined, pioneering, aggressive.**

2 Two is the first soul plane number. It represents our dualistic nature as spiritual beings in a physical body. The two represents our need to find balance between these two opposing sides of ourselves. Two is the number of intuition, sensitivity and cooperation. **Keywords: contrast, balance, cooperation, sensitive, intuitive, supportive, co-dependent.**

3 Three is the first mind plane number. As the imaginative yet rational and analytical number, it represents left-brain activity. Three is the number of imagination and memory and is particularly linked to the numbers one and two. Three's expression is directly tied to the intuitive and sensitive energy of the two and the verbal expression of the one. Three is symbolic of the mind (three), body (one), and soul (two) connection. **Keywords: analytical, intelligent, humorous, social, sensitive, observant, critical.**

4 Four is the middle physical plane number. It represents stability, steady progress, practicality, and organization. It is the anchor of the physical plane and is represented by the solid and stable construction of the square with its four equal sides. It is the most primitive of numbers. **Keywords: endurance, progress, foundation, practical,**

organization, solid, stable, materialistic.

5 Five is the middle soul plane number and is also the central number on the birth chart. Five symbolizes the heart/emotions and as the center number, links the energies of all the other numbers. It is the heart and soul of the birth chart. Five must have freedom to express itself as by nature, it is an erratic, free-flowing energy pattern. The five energy lends us the ability to see the world through the eyes of the soul. **Keyword: loving, sensitive, irregular, artistic, freedom-seeking, passionate, uncertain.**

6 Six is the middle Mind Plane number. It links both the three (left-brain) and the nine (right-brain). It is the number of extremes with both a strong positive and negative side. Six has an enormous amount of creative potential as the number of creativity. When not positively creating, it can slip into the opposite (and negative) side of creativity … destruction. In the negative, six is dominated by worry, anxiety and other negative thought patterns. In the positive, six can act as the "balancer" of the mind plane with its responsible, nurturing, and peace-maker qualities. **Keywords: creative, responsible, nurturing, home-loving, peace-maker, doting, worry-wart, people-pleaser, hostess, gossipy.**

7 Seven is the last and most active physical plane number. As the teaching/learning number, it is high "doing" energy. Seven learns through personal experience (often through hindsight), preferring to leap first and think later. Sacrifice and loss tend to be the rule of thumb for the seven energy. Such learning sets the stage for the accumulation of a tremendous amount of knowledge and wisdom in a short amount of time, making seven the self-made wise sage. **Keywords: wise, contemplative, achiever, determined, stubborn, active.**

8 Eight is the last and most active soul plane number. It represents wisdom and independence. Eight is confident, assertive, naturally wise and very much a leadership energy. Yet, at the same time, eight is loving and tender. These conflicting aspects of the eight energy create its main lesson—to learn to recognize that openly expressing love and appreciation will not subtract from independence, but add to it. **Keywords: independent, wise leader, loving, assertive, confident, dynamic, detached, selfish.**

9 Nine is the last and most active mind plane number. Although nine represents the right brain, it also combines the attributes of the other two mind plane numbers, three and six. Ambition (three), responsibility (six) and idealism (nine) make up the whole essence of the nine energy. Despite the idealistic and driven nature of the nine, it is a seeker of peace and justice and is considered the humanitarian number. **Keywords: humanitarian, ambitious, responsible, justice-seeking, idealistic, unselfish, driven, opinionated, judgmental.**

0 Zero is not a number but a symbol of the infinite. It symbolizes nothing and everything—energy not yet manifested into the physical. Zero represents our spiritual potential. Those with one or more zeros in their date of birth have an inherent spiritual awareness, waiting to be brought to full fruition. When a zero shows up in a numerical message, it highlights the importance or urgency of the message. The more zeros, the more important the message is.

With a firm understanding of your own energies and expression of them, you're ready to move on to relationships and how your own life path and lesson plan may intertwine with a significant other.

CHAPTER 10:
RELATIONSHIPS: TRANSLATION (NOT COMPATIBILITY) IS KEY

Significantly Improve Relationship Connections by Learning to Speak Their Vibrational Language

If you often feel misunderstood in a relationship, it likely isn't a compatibility issue; it is more a case of misunderstanding. Do you feel frustrated with your partner because you don't understand their views? What if you could speak their language?

Kids are a totally different ball game. Or are they? Most parents wish their child came with an owner's manual, but in fact, most child/parent relationships are a result of simple misunderstanding. Through learning about the underlying vibrational energies that make up our world and those in it, misunderstanding turns into clarity. When we shine a light on and begin to understand the differences of others, we gain patience and appreciation where there was originally confusion and frustration. You may have a temper-tantrum toddler or a teen that seems to be growing apart from the family or, worse still, becoming that dreaded wild-child you feared. If you can't seem to meet eye-to-eye, there's a solution to understanding your teen, tween, or child. All the answers are contained in their date of birth.

Simply by analyzing their birth date you can crack open the mind and soul of the person you want to understand. It gives you the tools to speak their language. Most relationship trouble stems from not understanding the differences of others. The classic nagging wife and tuned-out husband are really a case of a mental-based person paired with a physical-based person. Approaching someone from their perspective significantly improves communication and understanding.

Once you intimately know the differences of the other person, you can appreciate them. Frustration is replaced by patience, understanding, and clear communication.

Anything I speak of in this book is not just a result of regurgitating numerology information. I would never teach a theory that I haven't tried myself. The relationship work proved incredibly accurate and helpful for me starting with my daughter. At the age of one and a half, she began taking up to two hour temper-tantrums. While she was writhing on the floor, my toddler was inconsolable and unreachable. Sometimes her fits would be so prolonged and severe that she would urinate and defecate in her pants. I thought I was the most horrible mother on the planet, and that her behavior was a result of my poor parenting. These fits started happening around the same time I began dreaming in numbers every night.

One of my first ah-ha moments was when I discovered that my daughter had the Arrow of High Expectations on her Birth Chart. What a weight lifted when I realized it was her energetic makeup causing the tantrums and behavioral issues. I wasn't a bad mother after all. I instantly had more patience, appreciation, and understanding for my daughter. It completely changed our relationship.

Another big stepping stone in my relationship with my daughter happened when her pediatrician wanted to label her as a high-functioning autistic. He insisted that I send her for further analysis with a psychologist, and that he was certain they would confirm his initial diagnosis. My mother instinct screamed "No!" Had I not known what I did about her from a numerical and energetic standpoint, her life would likely be very different right now if I followed through with the in-depth diagnosis. In our case, it turned out that it was best that we followed the non-medical approach to her symptoms.

From a numerological perspective, she not only had double twos, the number of intuition and sensitivity, but the Arrow of High Expectations, which caused her to set the bar extremely high in terms of expectations of herself and others. Once I addressed this issue, I found a big reduction in her outbursts, and that it was a big cause of the temper tantrums and inadaptable behaviors. She was unable to shift gears when things didn't go as she saw them to be in her mind. Stuck in the disappointment of the situation, she needed help to see an alternative perspective.

Presently, she is in fourth grade and doing well in school and socially well adjusted. I'll admit she's a bit eccentric and is more artistically than academically inclined, according to her numerology profile, but in my parental opinion, I don't believe her to be autistic in the textbook sense of the label. I shudder to think about how many children could be helped in alternative ways as my daughter has been instead being given the drug treatments.

Interestingly, a trend I've noticed in my own numerological practice is the number of kids diagnosed with ADHD. I believe that this is due to the fact that these children were born in the late 1990s, which mean they have multiple nines in their birth dates. The nine is the most active mental number and very out-of-the-box, idealistic thinking kind of energy.

The second wave of children labeled as autistic being seem to be have started entering the scene starting in the early 2000s. These children typically have multiple twos in their date of birth, the number of intuition and sensitivity. Instead of being hyperactive, like the previous ADHD group, this new wave of children seem more passive, sensitive to everything from food to clothing labels, and emotionally unpredictable. The two is the most sensitive and cooperative of all the soul-based number patterns. It is a pattern I will continue to watch as my own children fit within the latter category of traits. I have used this knowledge in my own parenting tactics with great success.

Knowing that my daughter has multiple twos (number of intuition and sensitivity) has helped me to remain more patient and understanding when I heard the words "It doesn't feel right" for the tenth time in one day related to anything from the texture of food to the tags on clothing. When she loses it on the front steps because some little thing went wrong at school that day, I know that she has the traits of the Arrow of High Expectations which causes her to set the bar too high in terms of her expectations. Knowledge of these inner qualities of Rileigh allows me to be a better parent and lessen frustration for both of us. It has truly changed my life as a parent.

Everyone born in the 1900s has at least one nine in their date of birth. Being the number of ambition and idealism, it's no wonder we saw such progress and achievement in the previous century like no other time in history. In essence, we all carry some of that unrelenting spunk and restless mental energy these "hyperactive" children seem to possess so we "get" them to some degree.

Two energy, on the other hand, is vastly different from the nine energy we're used to. It is the most sensitive soul plane number while nine is the most active mental number. This is the most misunderstood group, and, and, as in the case of my own daughter, is a prime example of how successful relationships can be achieved by understanding the differences of others. It is imperative we learn to communicate with them from their perspective.

Whether is it your partner, child, friend, parent, or boss, you can shift a dysfunctional relationship in an instant simply by gaining an understanding their energetic makeup. Life is all about the perspective you hold, and this is especially true in relationships. A grudge can easily melt into forgiveness when you know how the other person operates from the inside out.

When analyzing the numbers of those you hold relationships with, you'll want to look for the same things you would when examining your own energetic patterns. Things like which plane of existence are their numbers most clustered on (are they a feeler, thinker, or doer?). This will tell you, for starters, what language they're speaking. If you're a thinker and your teen is a feeler, it could explain why they think you have too many rules, and why you think they're an impulsive wild-child. Thinkers rationalize decisions while feelers make decisions based on how it feels. Also, compare Life Theme Numbers, as this is the first point of comparison. If one of you is a nine (idealistic mental number) and the other a five (number of heart representing freedom of expression), there's challenge number one.

Trying to find similarities between a mental energy (ex. a nine) with a soulful energy (ex. a five) is like comparing oil and water. They each view life from a very different perspective. When you analyze the numerological profile of another, you are able to see the world through their eyes and understand how they operate. Understanding the traits and qualities of another is the most important part. You can't change someone else, you can only change yourself. It isn't your job to do that. Your job is to understand who and why others are in your life. The interactions we have with others are a big part of our life lessons. There may be a deeper meaning that lies within your connection to another which can be revealed through analyzing their date of birth, comparing it to the qualities you have in yours. Is your unruly and mouthy teen in your life to teach you how to communicate? It's worth your while to start with discovering the main essence of all involved. It's the first step to understanding the energies you're working through.

Next, you'll want to look for number imbalances. For example, as the verbal self expression number, a single one (most balanced is double ones) indicates difficulty with expressing emotions. Isolated numbers are another challenge in relationships because they do just what the names says—isolate in some form. Isolated mental numbers lead to miscommunication of thoughts and ideas while isolated physical numbers can lead to repeating the same patterns and experiences that cause sacrifice, loss, and hardship.

Another area we can look for is any strengths and challenge areas (Arrows of Pythagoras). For example, if you're missing all three soul plane numbers (Arrow of Emotional Sensitivity), you may find yourself attracting partners who will either be emotionally distant or eventually hurt you. Emotionally sensitive people tend to put up walls to protect their heart, keeping others at arm's length. The partners they often attract will usually be someone who doesn't mind being held at a distance because they are also emotionally unavailable.

Highlighting and comparing these areas on the two birth charts will show you not only where you need to grow in a relationship, but it also gives you clear explanations as to why the ones you care for never seem to meet eye to eye.

Since I talked a bit about my own relationship challenges in the beginning of this chapter, let's take a closer look at this mother/daughter relationship and the challenges we faced right from the get-go. As a primer, I'll say that we're both a Life Theme Number three, but as you'll see, we're almost polar opposites.

Here is my daughter Rileigh's chart:

Mind Plane		↑	
Soul Plane	22		
Physical Plane	1		7

As you can see, she is ultra emotionally sensitive with double twos (number of intuition and sensitivity), has a difficult time expressing how she feels with a single one (unbalanced verbal self-expression), an isolated seven (repeating of the same life lessons and experiences), and the Arrow of High Expectations (has unrealistically high expectations for herself and others).

Now here's a look at my chart for comparison:

Mind Plane			↑9
Soul Plane			8
Physical Plane	11	4	7 →

In contrast, I'm lacking the more sensitive numbers on the chart and have only the eight on the soul plane, which is the strongest and least sensitive emotional-based number. I've never understood my daughter's hypersensitive nature completely, although I try my best to be patient with her sensitivities. It is definitely a growth area for me, as I've never been particularly touchy-feely or emotionally sensitive.

Where I have the Arrow of Practical Action, my daughter is lacking the grounded, practical number four. I have the hardest time dealing with everything being apocalyptic in Rileigh's world. Her impractical and sensitive nature makes it easy for her to lose control and become frantic over simple things like misplacing her favorite shirt. Her Arrow of High Expectations adds to the pot, bringing even more unrealistic expectations of herself and others into the equation. My rational and extra practical side (with all three physical plane numbers) says she's being a complete diva. This is my most challenging area in this relationship connection and where I find I have the least amount of patience.

Lastly, I have the Arrow of Great Expression, and when this energy combines with my Arrow of Practical Action, I'm a total "doer." My daughter, on the other hand, has just as much emotional energy as physical. This means her sensitive side usually overrides any semblance of physical energy she might carry. The older she gets, the lazier she is, and listening to music wins out over cleaning her room or doing chores. She's easily distracted by sights and sounds that excite her emotionally sensitive nature.

In summary, you can see clearly that my relationship with my first born is chalk-full of life lessons for the both of us. When opposites attract in relationships, it's usually because one person has what the other is lacking. In the case of my daughter and me, by observing her, she is teaching me so much about the sensitive side of life. I'm teaching her that real life also includes taking action on your dreams and goals. From an energetic perspective, we balance each other completely. This is often the scenario in many of our closer connections in life such as mother/father, sister/brother, child/parent, partner/spouse. These relationships will usually contain the most challenges, but also the most learning points.

The information contained within this chapter is important for you to explore, because at the basis of why we are all here is to interact with others. At the core, regardless of whether you are a poet or an accountant, our path and purpose involves being of service to others in some way. Unless your purpose is to spend your entire life in a cave alone, your relationships will play a significant part of who/ what you become. Although life is about the free-will choices we make, the interactions we have with other people shapes and shifts the trajectory of those choices on many levels.

Knowing the significance and energetic components of the people you choose to be in a relationship with can shed an even brighter light on your path, purpose, and destiny.

CHAPTER 11: YOUR HOUSE COULD BE HOLDING YOU BACK

The Energy of a Home or Business Can Have a Significant Impact on Your Health and Success

An address, like everything in existence, has an energy all its own and can have a significant influence on us. Have you ever considered that your health challenges are aggravated by your home's energetic vibration, or that your toxic work environment might be more than just a result of the office drama? Energy can be complimentary with our own energetic essence, or rub us the wrong way, creating "static" in our lives. This includes the energy of the place we spend our time. It allows this energy to have influence. Is your home compatible with your energy?

Analyzing an address can tell you whether the property is compatible with you or anyone else who spends a great deal of time there. Some address numbers are good for business and financial prosperity yet not so great for your love life. Others may not be ideal for building a family unit but perfect for if you appreciate time alone. Some addresses inspire and uplift while others encourage you to spend time in self-reflection mode.

Depending on your own energetic make-up, your house could be complimentary, or it could hinder your success. House energy can also affect not only our ability to accomplish but your overall well-being. Finding a house that fits us is very important because a building we spend a lot of time in can act as an energetic catalyst in the positive or the negative.

Over time, you may find that you have outgrown your house, and it is time to move on. This can happen, for example, if you spent time working on inner growth in a two or seven house and now find yourself drawn to settle down and start a family. Two or seven house energies aren't particularly great for families but better suited to single people (or couple) seeking spiritual growth and solitude. The four or eight provides a stable and foundational home for families, as four represents the square and its four sides. The eight encourages financial stability and is perfect for a home-based business.

Of course there are endless options for the vast array of unique energy combinations. For some families, a two or seven house may work perfectly. This is especially true if all members of the household value their alone time regularly, as both frequencies are self-reflective and isolating.

In our early twenties, my husband and I bought our first house. We thought we were the coolest, buying a ski chalet near Crabbe Mountain, a ski resort on the East Coast of Canada. Little did we know that house had a lot more to it than just being trendy.

Unfortunately, at that time in my life, it was before I had learned anything about numbers, numerology or energy. In hindsight, I now understand why that house seemed to give us so much grief. The sum of the address was a 16/7, which is a very volatile, inner change and truth-revealing energy (the word hate vibrates to this frequency). It pushes you to go within to accomplish profound inner work and shifting. In our early twenties, we were hardly ready for such deep spiritual growth. Needless to say, over the few years we were there, we found the house growing increasing uncomfortable, but we never could put our finger on why. We were on edge, fought more, felt restless and agitated, and didn't recognize who we were anymore. By the fourth year, we put the house up for sale, and we were prepared to walk away if we didn't sell it right away. That's how badly we wanted to get away from that spiritually invasive house. Thankfully, we sold it very quickly because it was time for us to move on.

As you can see from my example, a house can really wreak havoc on your life. I'm a firm believer that everything happens for a reason, and I'm sure my husband and I gleaned many things from the experiences. I won't be buying a 16/7 house anytime soon. This particular house frequency (16/7) has a tendency to be a transitional house where people move in specifically because they need to go through a transformational or deeper truth-revealing experience, and then they move on. They aren't aware of this consciously, but their soul draws them to the house's energy to learn particular life lessons (the house acts as a catalyst).

The next time you're in the market for a new pad, you may be initially drawn to the location, paint color, or layout of the property, but now you'll have a new tool to help you decide what space is right for you. Ultimately go with your intuition, because you might need a certain house for reasons yet to be revealed (like I did). Remember, numbers are a guide to the energy and not the end-all-be-all of decision making. For example, don't avoid a "nesting" six address because you aren't yet ready to start a family. There may be other relationship issues that need work, and if you're really drawn to that six house, it may be optimum for you at that time.

There are three different ways to analyze an address. The street number is the number which resonates most with us and is considered the most important aspect of an address's vibration. When calculating the street number's numerical meaning, always reduce to a single digit. For example, 465 Bistro Avenue would be added as 4+6+5=15, further reduces to 1+5=6.

Another way to look at the details of a location's energy is to examine the individual digits in the street address. The individual numbers exert a lesser influence than the sum of the digits, but they still play a role in the property's overall energetic pattern. This is especially so if the street address has multiples of the same digit like 1115, 222, 339, 8884, etc.

Examining an address in this way is similar to analyzing our birth dates or Birth Charts. The overall sum of the digits is the house's main essence (like our Life Theme Number), and the individual numbers are like the traits/tools (individual numbers on Birth Chart, strengths/weaknesses).

The third way to view a property's energetic pattern is to add the entire address, including both the street number of the house, and the numerical value of the words in the street name. This is a much broader view of the property's energy as there are many Bistro Avenues in the world. By far, the most important and most relevant number is the street or house number reduced to a single digit, but there are always exceptions to the rule. You may find that your property resonates most with the overall total frequency of the address (numbers and words). For instance, this can sometimes be the case with unusual/unique street names.

To calculate your own property's essence, begin by adding the street number and reduce to a single digit. The meanings of each address number from one to nine are listed on the following pages. When looking at the street digits individually, refer to each separate number meaning to discover the different elements of the house's energetic makeup. For example, 123 Main Street has the overall essence of six (1+2+3=6) but also carries the qualities of the one, two and three.

When calculating the total of both the street number and street name, refer to the Name Conversion Chart in Chapter below, which gives the numerical value for each letter in the alphabet. Use the full street name including the suffix (street, avenue, road, lane, etc). Add the letter values to the street number and reduce to a single digit.

NAME CONVERSION CHART

1	2	3	4	5	6	7	8	9
A	B	C	D	E	F	G	H	I
J	K	L	M	N	O	P	Q	R
S	T	U	V	W	X	Y	Z	

Continuing with our first example of 465 Bistro Avenue, we already calculated the street number (4+6+5=6) and now let's reduce the street name to numerical values:

B	I	S	T	R	O
2	9	1	2	9	6

A	V	E	N	U	E
1	4	5	5	3	5

2+9+1+2+9+6+1+4+5+5+3+5=**52**

Now add the street number calculation (6) to the street name total (7) to get final base energy:

(street number) 6 + 7 (street name) = 13

Reduce further to a single digit: 1+3=4

In the above example, the house energy is a four. This third way of analyzing an address is a broad view and should not be used as the primary method of determining compatibility of a property. It's fun to see what this number adds to, but it should be viewed more like our Complete Name Number. Our name is not our true essence but rather how we express ourselves through our "mask" or personality expression. Likewise, by adding the numerical meaning of both the street number and name, we get a view of the personality energies of the house, not its true essence.

This method of calculating energetic patterns can also be applied to a car's license plate number/letter combination. In the hustle-bustle cities of today, we can spend a large portion of our day stuck in traffic. What energetic influence does your car have on you? Convert the letters to numerical form, add all the numbers together and reduce to a single digit. Refer to the main base number meanings in Chapter three to interpret the meaning.

Below are the main address number meanings from one to nine. It can also be enlightening to go back in time to calculate the addresses of previous homes you've resided in and pair the energies with the experiences you went through. This will allow you to see if you were influenced by the property itself.

ADDRESS NUMBER MEANINGS 1-9

1 Great for singles with career/business as top priority, not good for wishy-washy unmotivated people. One is the number of ego expression through verbal means and as such, the one property is confident and assertive. This address is all about achievement through physically doing and experiencing.

Keywords: **New beginnings/opportunities, independence, leadership, determination/drive, spontaneous, impulsive.**

2 The two energy brings a peaceful, harmonious and sensitive atmosphere and is great for inspiring romance. A good choice for couples, but singles may find it lonely and isolating as it is an intimate energy. Great address for social events such as family reunions where coming together or "union" energy is wanted. The two is not really driven energy but rather a thoughtful and supportive one.

Keywords: Supportive, sensitive, intuitive, loving, marriage, cooperation, team work, patience.

3 Good address for both families and singles. Lacks focus, direction and motivation but inspires creativity. "Dreamers" and inspirational people, such as artists and authors, are best suited to a three property. The ambitious or career-driven should avoid this property. The three address loves social gatherings, visitors, and parties of all kinds.

Keywords: Bright, happy, casual, social, fun-loving, not serious, humorous, creative, optimistic, flexible, happy-go-lucky.

4 The four house is a place where a family can feel truly at home, safe and secure. A four address works very well when a "home-base" feeling is required. Not a great house for artistic or eccentric people, and is better suited to young families needing financial stability and a place lay down a foundation. Career-oriented singles also do well in a four address because it encourages financial growth and practicality.

Keywords: Solid, secure, stable, predictable, practical, home-base, conventional, responsible, trustworthy, foundation.

5 This is a heart-centered address. A great address for singles looking for love, but it lacks the stability to grow and nurture a long-term connection. Emotions can run high in a five house. Those with an even Life Theme Number can find the energy of a five house too chaotic and erratic to live in long-term. This is an ideal spot for the artistic/eccentric single, but if you're looking to start a family or build a stable foundation in life, it may be best to choose an even number address.

Keywords: Beauty, love, passion, freedom, change, romance, unreliable, unstable, impulsive, risk-taking.

6 This address competes with the four for the perfect family home. The six encourages the sharing of feelings and doesn't allow relationship issues to fester. It is a very nurturing environment, a place where strong bonds can form—a place to nurture and be nurtured. Six is more passionate and feeling than the practical four house, so if you're prone to anxiety or stress, a four location would suite you better. Six is the number of creativity, so it is a great location for any career or business involving creative expression.

Keywords: Responsible, loving, creative, idealistic, nurturing, family, relationships, sharing.

7 An ideal home for independent singles or families with older, more self-sufficient children. The seven address strongly encourages inner growth through personal experience (often involving hindsight learning). The seven home is best for the person who likes to have adequate alone time to self-reflect. As much as the seven address encourages leaping before thinking, it also emphasizes the need to seek the deeper meaning of life as it is the truth-seeker number. Those who like to keep life light and fun will find the seven address too serious and deep. Coincidentally, many churches are located at a seven address. Not a good address for a business unless it is spiritually-oriented.

Keywords: Personal experience, hindsight, challenges, opportunities, confrontations, dynamics, exciting, unconventional, contemplation, inner growth, introversion.

8 This is the perfect location for a business but of the more serious kind (not of a spiritual or artistic nature as eight energy is normally quite conventional). Eight energy encourages financial growth and stability, and therefore is a great place for both singles and families with financial growth/stability as a top focus. The energy of an eight location is strong and enduring which can lead to a strengthening of the mental and physical bodies while living there. Top choices for the eight home are career-driven people or larger families.

Keywords: Serious, business, deep change, opportunities, wealth, achievement, financial growth, confidence, stability, authority, drive.

9 Since the nine is a mental number, idealism rules in a nine location. Dreamers and idealists thrive in the nine property. We can see the broader picture of life from a nine location and a good helping of deep thinking and planning goes on there. However, it isn't the best location to grow financially, as the idealistic ideas are usually missing the finer details required to bring the plan to life. The nine represents the end of a cycle, which can also create a calm and serene atmosphere depending upon the essence of the people who live there. Better suited to singles—serious and more career-driven people should avoid a nine location. An excellent home to retire in or reflect on life and can also be a financially lucky address.

Keywords: Idealism, personal growth, self-confidence, serious, compassionate, humanitarian, change, intellectual, productive.

Phone Numbers

Whether it's your business line or personal cell, a phone number exerts its own energetic influence on us. In business, it can mean the difference between attracting customers or sending them away. What frequency are people dialing when they call you? If you want people to feel stability and loyalty, go with a number that adds to a four. If you want them to feel as though you have the answers they are seeking, choose a seven.

A phone number is by far the least influential compared to the Life Theme Number or Heart's Desire Number. However, sometimes even small changes like a phone number can help to shift certain energy patterns in your life, so it's worth the effort to take a look at it.

A phone number is analyzed in much the same way as an address. The full seven digit phone number is too broad since many people share the area code and the first three digits (just as many people share the same street name). The last four digits of your phone number are unique to you. To calculate the energy of a phone number, add the last four digits together and reduce to a single digit like this: ***-***-**8231**, 8+2+3+1=14, 1+4=**5**. In this example, the energetic pattern being dialed into when someone calls it is the five.

The individual numbers can also be looked at separately, particularly if there are interesting combinations like multiples of the same number or several zeros.

To get a feel for the meaning of your phone number's vibration, review the address meanings and also look back at the base number meanings (one to nine) as well as the Life Theme Number meanings. For example, a four is a four is a four no matter if it is a Life Theme Number, a name, or a phone number. The four will always carry the traits of practicality and stability no matter where you see it.

After reading this chapter, you'll start to look at inanimate things and their influence on your life a whole lot differently. All things in existence carry an energetic frequency that can influence other interacting energies. Energy flows until it encounters resistance. Your house and phone number are just two of the inanimate objects that could be complimenting or creating friction with your own energy, thus impeding the unfolding of your life's master plan. The objective is to keep the energetic flow of life going smoothly with the least amount of resistance.

That said, there are times when we need friction to create life experiences for learning, and that can sometimes mean choosing a house that rubs us the wrong way or a phone number that attracts the wrong kinds of people. Life boils down to the choices we make, and at the end of the day, there's no right or wrong path. We can, however, make better selections when we're armed with the appropriate knowledge. Awareness of the energies within and around us means the difference between taking the easy commute or going the long, scenic route. We should enjoy the journey of life and not be just focused on the destination. But that doesn't mean we can't make the journey more fun and enjoyable by being aware of the energies that influence us along the way and know how to work with them to create less friction for a smoother ride.

CHAPTER 12: NUMERICAL MESSAGES FROM BEYOND

Seeing Repeating Number Patterns Everwhere?
These Are Messages from the Realm of Energy.

Have you ever had the same number or number sequences appear everywhere such as on clocks, signs, in dreams, etc? There could be a message waiting for you in those numbers. Our soul attempts to communicate with us in ways we will hear the messages and that can include numbers.

Globally, there are also messages in numbers. These may be events that occur on specific dates. Even still, they could be the birth dates of world leaders. Either way, these numbers can combine and impact our lives through their energetic patterns.

Take for example the global financial crisis. The previous century, with every person having at least one instance of nine and one in their date of birth, carried the ambitious, idealistic, and big dreamer energy of the nine and the pioneering, trailblazing, and egocentric one. It's no wonder we saw such progress and achievement during that time. Such combined ambition built global energy to an all-time high, and we saw the money, power, greed model immerging. Now we are witnessing the subsequent crash and burn of that empire in the form of the financial crisis. As we moved into the subdued 2000s, we have yet to see the same level of achievement reached in the current century.

Here are the messages behind the numbers: The tragedy of 9-11 was the first marker of the spiraling financial crisis. I can remember even my own husband lost his job as a mechanic shortly after this act of terrorism. It crippled the world, and we all held our breath for sometime afterward. This marker event happened in the ninth month, the highest change month of the year, the word "money" adds to nine, the words "Wall Street" add to nine, the word "east" adds to nine (where Wall Street is). The hurricane named Sandy that demolished much of the Jersey Shore added to a nine. It may be just a coincidence that all of these things are a nine frequency, or there may be a deeper message that we need to shift our focus away from the money, power, and greed energy, which grips our current civilization.

What about the 11:11 phenomenon where so many people globally were reporting seeing this particular time sequence on clocks regularly? It is associated with the Mayans, and this number is throughout their writings, linking it to the "end of times" date that has come and gone.

As we struggle globally to get a handle on finances, the United States recently had in the running for the last election a Life Theme Number nine (Mitt Romney) and a Life Theme Number eleven (Barack Obama). The nine is the very energy we need to leave in the past, as it represents black-and-white judgmental and idealistic thinking of the previous century. Eleven is the new spiritual energy that is not focused on money, power, or greed. Ironically, a leader of a nation who carries the eleven and puts money last is the very thing we need to focus on to fixing the money crisis. Obama was in office for four years prior, and as a Spiritual Guide (11/2), his energy was meant to act as support (2) during the fall of the financial structures. Had an ambitious, idealistic, and justice-seeking nine been in power at that time, the financial crisis may have been fueled further by such drive and determination. Nines often have the blinders on, charging full-steam ahead and missing the finer, yet crucial details.

Money cannot dominate us any longer if we are to move forward successfully as a planet. Money needs to be recognized as a tool only, and that we (and not money) are truly the creators of our own reality. The financial crisis could be viewed as an outward representation of the ego side of ourselves dominating our true nature as a spiritual being. Like the mind, our ego (personality) is a tool for the soul and not meant to lead us. We have forgotten who we really—a soul in human form. Numerology is a powerful tool of self-discovering to help us recognize the areas out of balance and assist us in realigning. When centered in our soulful self, we are in control of our own reality, not any person, place or thing (including money).

Is it a coincidence that a Life Theme Number nine (Romney) lost the election to a Life Theme Number eleven (Obama)? Obama and his wife Michelle are both a Life Theme Number eleven. Could they be the 11:11 pair to lead us into the New Age of peace, harmony, and cooperation that has been predicted by the Mayans?[12]

From a Biblical perspective, the name Jesus is an eleven who was a man that led by kindness, generosity, and unconditional love— certainly not by money, power, or greed. Our name is how the world views us, and the world saw Jesus as someone who let his soul lead his actions. The message of the eleven showing up with such frequency right now is a message of the shift toward the need to begin living in alignment with our soulful self once again.

The above example of hidden meanings behind the numbers is just one scenario. There are endless numerical patterns and messages bombarding us all the time—if we're willing to pay attention to them.

On a personal note, the story of how my son was conceived seems very accidental on the exterior. However, the numbers associated with his birth reveal a deeper meaning. When my daughter was about one and a half years old, I went to see a very gifted medium that came highly recommended. My deceased grandmother came through that day and delivered the message of congratulations. The medium proceeded to tell me that my grandmother was not elaborating on why she was congratulating me. At the time, I didn't put much thought into it because I was already married. I had adamantly decided there would be no other children after having my difficult first child, so I was unclear as to why I was being congratulated.

A few years later my husband was on the vasectomy list waiting for a surgery date when I discovered I was pregnant. I was diligent in preventing another pregnancy, and yet it happened somehow.

When my son was born, he weighed seven pounds seven ounces. After I came home from the hospital, one of the first books I consulted was Doreen Virtue's "Angel Numbers 101," which says multiple sevens mean congratulations.

There are many ways you can analyze number sequences, and the same number can mean different things to different people.

The best part is you have the nine Base Number Meanings that you've already learned in chapter three, which will allow you to be able to analyze *any* number sequence presented to you at the base level. We're also going to look a little deeper into the vibration of a number pattern.

To analyze a number in its totality, you need to look at each number sequence in three ways: The individual number meanings, the sum of the digits before reducing to a single digit, and the base number after reducing. All three have their own layer of messages that are contained within the number pattern.

For example, triple eights is a repeat of the number of wisdom and independence. With triple doubtless wisdom power, this sequence says you should feel confident in your decisions and actions. Added together, it is twenty-four, which combine the energies of intuition (2) and practical action (4). Finally, when reduced, it is the creative visionary six (2+4=6). As we are responsible for creating our own reality, this number sequence really stresses that you need not worry as your soul (2) is in charge of guiding your actions (4) to manifest all that you desire.

The science of numbers teaches that we should always reduce any number to its base number, meaning from one to nine. While it's true that the most important information comes from understanding the base energies of a person, place, or thing, additional information can be derived from working with the sum of a date of birth *before* it is reduced to the singular. This includes number sequences of any kind.

If for example a date of birth added to thirty-two and 3+2=5, we know this person has the Life Theme Number five. However, they are actually working with the energies of the three, the two, and the five. How does each of these individual numbers affect the trajectory, purpose, and outlook of the Life Theme Number five? Let's find out!

Continuing with our example of the 32/5 Life Theme Number, let's break it down further:

The outer number (3) is considered the greatest strength, and the inner number (2) is considered the greatest challenge area. When consulting the base number meanings for any number sequence, typically the positive traits for the strength position number (outer) are relevant as are the more negative traits for the weaker position number (inner).

Some number sequences or Life Theme Number examples may add to two separate double digit numbers before reducing to the final base number, like this: 39/12/3. When you get a date of birth or a number sequence that adds in this way, you will need to look at both pairs of double digit values as there may be two main strength and two main weakness areas.

If you arrive at a Master Number, refer to the Master Number meanings (chapter three) before dividing the energies up into the main strength/weakness. For example, the Master Number 33/6 has double hurdles to jump through with the double threes, which is why many 33/6 (like Lindsay Lohan) tend to self-sabotage. Although the three is imaginative, creative, and inspirational, the negative side of the three can be self-doubt, self-critical and irrational. When the 33/6 gets in a negative space, those uplifting and inspiring threes can create double challenge hoops for them to jump through before being able to access their create six energy.

Use your best judgment and intuition when analyzing number patterns or sequences. You may be working the energies in the positive or negative or a combination of both. It is often essential to examine your entire numerological chart first before trying to decipher what the number message contains for you.

This arena of analyzing number messages is becoming a phenomenon worldwide, and many people are reporting seeing peculiar repeating numbers everywhere they go. In my own life, I became intrigued by seeing number sequences when I began seeing 11:11 every day on clocks, license plates, in phone numbers, and in countless other synchronistic places. While stopped at a red light, I happened to look up at an awning over a business and the address was 1111. When I reached for my cell phone to take a picture of it, my phone time display was 1:11pm. Whenever I see either 1:11 or 11:11, I get an overwhelming of assurance that what I am focusing my attention on is the right thing and to keep going. Numerically speaking, the one is the pioneer energy and the first physical number representing verbal self-expression. In multiples, the one stresses the need and urgency to take physical action (with a focus on verbal action). The 1:11 adds to three, the number of inspired thinking, and 11:11 adds to four, the number of enduring effort, practical physical action and foundation building. Eleven is the highest spiritual number, and many who see multiple one messages are meant to guide others from a more soulful perspective. It is showing up so frequently now because the "guides" of the world are being called to their post to take action, as the world is in crisis on many levels. Based on my own experience with clients and other acquaintances, those who see 11:11 report feeling a sense of urgency and importance when they encounter it. Even though they might not be able to put their finger on what is urgent or important.

These kinds of numerical experiences happen to me all the time, and I'm honored to be able to help you make sense of the numbers that appear in your own life.

Below are the fifty-four patterns of creation. All things in existence are energy at the core and vibrate to one of these numerical patterns. Interestingly, 5+4=9, which represents that there are nine base energetic vibrations, even in the expanded view. Although only one of the base numbers represent the core of any energetic pattern, the expanded (non-reduced) version of a numerical pattern affords us a more intricate view of the messages they contain.

Whether it's a birth date or repeating digits on a clock, refer to this numerical meaning section to gain clarity of the message behind the numbers.

EXPANDED NUMBER MEANINGS
(54 PATHS OF CREATION)

1 1 is the first physical plane energy and is the pioneering, trailblazing number of new beginnings. As the verbal-self expression energy, it urges us to speak our mind, voice our views, and deliver information through verbal action.

Plane: Physical

Message: Take action, make changes, speak your mind, forge your own path, a new beginning is required or on its way.

10/1 Combining the energies of the verbal self-expression number (1) with the symbol of the infinite representing spiritual awareness, the 10/1 brings together the forces of heaven and earth. Called the Earth Guide, this energy leads us through casual conversation and gets in the trenches with the people rather than preaching from the mountain top. The 10/1 is known for having the one isolate the zero, creating a purely physical energy. For example, many who are a Life Theme Number ten will not delve into the spiritual side of themselves until they mature, focusing instead on the pioneering and action-packed one. When the 10/1 has a one-track mind, there is much accomplished and achieve in the physical sense, but there is always a feeling of longing for something more until the zero is integrated.

Plane: Physical/Soul

Message: Speak from the soul, voice your inner truths, don't hesitate to share wisdom gained from your life experiences.

2

2 is the number of intuition, sensitivity, peace, harmony, and cooperation. It is a dualistic energy that represents our spiritual and emotional sides. When tuned into our intuitive side, we have an inner sense of doubtlessness that everything is as it should be, regardless of what is going on in our life.

Plane: Soul (Gateway Number to Soul Plane)

Message: There is a need to trust your intuitive side more, everything is as it should be, you are safe, secure, and on path. Go with your gut and it will never steer you in the wrong direction.

20/2

The 20/2 carries all the qualities of the single two, such as intuition, sensitivity, peace, harmony, and cooperation. When combined with the zero, there is a spiritual urgency for you to focus on and embrace your spiritual side for guidance and direction.

Plane: Soul

Message: Pay attention to your inner voice, it is speaking to you. Pivotal decisions are upon you, and it is imperative you trust your intuition as it knows exactly what you need.

11/2

The 11/2 symbolizes the joining forces of body and soul. It is the spirit working through physical form as the double ones (physical plane) add to the number two (gateway number to soul plane). Referred to as the number of the Spiritual Guide, the 11/2 urges us to take action on what our intuition is telling us we need to do. Our soul has work to do in order to learn and evolve, and in the process of doing so, we assist others as well. The 11/2 is soulful guidance (2) through physical action (1). The 11/2 is one of the few energies that can fall victim to being way off the mark, even though at its base is the number of intuition (2). This is because the stand alone pioneering energy double one can dominate and isolate itself from the inner guiding compass of the soul. With this combination, the seat of all action needs to be based in the soulful side to remain balanced.

Plane: Physical/Soul

Message: You are being called to your post as guide, and it is time for you to lead by example. Follow your heart and intuition to embrace your soulful purpose and in doing so, you will lead others to their own path and purpose.

3 3 is the number of imagination, memory, inspiration, and unity. Intellectually based, it also forms the head of the Arrow of Spiritual Presence and Arrow of Inspiration. As creators of our own reality, we utilize the imaginative energy of the three as a pivotal tool in manifesting all that we desire.

Plane: Mind Plane

Message: Use the creative power of your imagination to unify your thoughts and focus in on precisely what you want to create in your life. Everything will come together as you desire.

12/3 The 12/3 is the "whole and complete" energy as twelve is the number of wholeness, and three is the number of unity. Your physical actions (1) are in alignment with your soul's desire (2) and are coming together beautifully (3). The 12/3 can become stuck when the negative traits of the two (co-dependence, uncertainty) put in on the fence and cloud the intuitive force behind the actions.

Plane: Physical/Soul/Mind

Message: Everything is coming full circle. You are remembering who you truly are, and all the forces of your being, mind, body, and soul are unifying into completeness. All that you have worked to achieve and the actions you have taken to focus on what your soul desires are paying off.

21/3 Opposite the previous number (12/3), the 21/3 has the two and the 1 reversed. Instead of focusing on your actions to manifest what your soul is urging you to accomplish, this combination wants you to focus more on the inner work to bring things into alignment. In this energetic pattern, the two is leading the way in the first position. The focus is soulful work which will guide you to the next steps. If the negative qualities of the one rear their head, it isolates the intuitive two, causing it to doubt what it feels. Staying centered in the intuitive self is essential to keeping the 21/3 balanced and in the flow.

Plane: Soul/Physical/Mind

Message: Let your intuition guide you at this time as everything will come together as you desire if you do.

30/3 Anytime a zero is paired with a number, it is highlighting the message. The pure three without any other number (zero is a symbol not a number) has a one-track mind focused on inspired imagination. We use the mind plane (the imagination) as a tool to bring our soul's desires to life.

Plane: Mind/Soul

Message: Pay attention to your thoughts. Your imagination (whether positive or negative) is rapidly manifesting what you are imagining. Be careful of a wandering mind falling victim to self-doubt and self-criticism.

4 The practical, solid, hard working, consolidating foundation number is all about building your empire from the ground up. The four is the number of the doer. It approaches life from a practical hands-on perspective. This allows you to roll up the sleeves and get the job done.

Plane: Physical

Message: It's important for you to take action toward building a solid foundation in your life. Begin consolidating the wisdom, knowledge, and resources available to you to begin building the life you desire.

13/4 Your imagination allows you to dream big and think outside the box, but to bring those ideas to fruition, you need to physically take action on them. Sandwiched between the pioneer number (1) and the solid foundation number (4), the energy of the imagination (3) has continuous physical momentum to bring ideas to life while in the positive. If it slips into the negative qualities of self-doubt and self-criticism, this four combination starts to become restless, impatient, and begins to lose momentum.

Plane: Physical/Mind

Message: Take action on the steps necessary to begin building what you've been dreaming and imagining for yourself. Steady action leads to making your dreams a reality.

22/4 22/4 is the Master Builder number that leads from a very involved standpoint. It is a practical energy (4) that is guided by heightened intuition (double 2). The double power of the two can overpower the four and step into its negative qualities of codependency, doubt and uncertainty creating a lopsided effect of doubting that the plan of action is the correct one. Re-centering in the intuitive self will shift the 22/4 back on course.

Plane: Soul/Physical

Message: You are intuitively in the zone with your actions and they are leading you onto your path toward purpose. Let your soul lead the way.

31/4 Inspired action is what the 31/4. The imagination (3) is the energetic engine behind the actions of the pioneer number (1) and the foundation building (4). This combination of the four is often the most doubt-filled as the one in the weaker (inner) position isolates the three. Sometimes pushing it into the negative qualities of self-doubt and self-criticism, it hinders inspiration.

Plane: Mind/Physical

Message: Let your imagination be the driving force behind your actions to successfully build your dreams.

40/4 The hardworking, practical and foundational four is highlighted and emphasized by the spiritual zero. The dreaming, analyzing, and planning is complete and the last step is to take action.

Plane:

Message: Follow your instincts and keeping going, you're almost there. You've put in the hard work and effort, and now you're at a place on the journey to start reaping the rewards through your actions.

5 As the number of the heart and emotions representing freedom of expression, the single five has a one track mind focused on following what the heart yearns for.

Plane: Soul

Message: Follow your heart and don't question it. The heart knows what it wants and needs. You are free to follow it completely.

14/5 At the basis of the 14/5 is the energy of the heart and emotions. It is an action-packed number with the most active physical plane numbers One and four leading the way but all actions are heart-centered (5). Since the four is in the weaker position, the impatient quality of the four can cause the 14/5 combination to lose steam and become frustrated if the goal is in the distance future.

Plane: Physical/Soul

Message: Follow your heart and act accordingly. Any action based on how it feels will lead you to where you need to be.

23/5 The 23/5 is the rarer form and most content (least freedom seeking) combination of the five. It is gentle natural counselor energy with intuition (2), imagination, and inspiration (3) combining to form the number of the heart (5). Relying on intuitive certainty and purely inspired thinking, this five is content to go with the flow of life knowing that all is as it should be. With the three in the weaker or less dominate position, the negative traits of the three can sometimes take hold (self-doubt, self-criticism) creating doubt-filled ideas. Refocusing on the doubtless intuitive two is essential to realign.

Plane: Soul/Mind

Message: You are right where you need to be, never doubt that. Your intuitive and imaginative powers are steering the chariot of your heart's desires. The sky is the limit; remember to keep believing that anything is possible.

32/5
This is the most bipolar form of the five with the inspirational three and the intuitive two battling forces when they slip into their negative form. In order to keep the imaginative three flowing, there is a delicate balance to maintain with the 32/5. If the two slips into uncertainty (negative form), the three shifts from inspiration to doubt. When off track, this five becomes self-doubting, uncertain, moody, and controlling.

Plane: Mind/Soul

Message: Your heart and soul believe in your inspired dreams 100%. Stay centered on your ideas, following the ones that feel right in your heart, even if they may seem overly grand. You are a limitless creator and can bring anything into reality you can imagine for yourself.

41/5
This freedom-seeking five has the enduring work horse four driving the car with the pioneering, trailblazing one acting as the fuel behind the expression of the five. This action-packed combination of the heart-centered five is the epitome of the soul in action. Practical, patient, and steady, the expression with the 41/5 is endless, unless the isolating one dips into the negative and cuts off the fuel supply. Care needs to be taken not to allow the double physical energies of the one and four to overpower the number of the heart (5).

Plane: Physical/Soul

Message: You are an unstoppable expressive force who acts solely upon only your soul's truest desires. Your body and soul are working in harmony to create your reality.

50/5
When paired with the deeply spiritual symbol of the infinite, the five is all about love and soulful expression. This strictly

soul-based five combination works predominantly with one main energy (5), making it a pure vibration. This is the central focus—heart-centered freedom of expression. Behind all actions of the passionate and loving, 50/5 is to create and express in a way that stirs the heart and soul. If the zero is cut off, this five can become trapped in the erratic negative energy of the five. Emotions are up and down, and intuition is clouded. Consultation with the inner self on a regular basis is imperative to keeping this free-flowing energy streaming in the positive.

Plane: Soul

Message: You are free to express yourself following only your heart and emotions as the guide.

6 The single six is the creative, nurturing energy which focuses on creative expression. As the number of extremes, the single six can be prone to pessimism and criticalness, doubting the tremendous creative power it holds. Continually moving forward and keeping the creative juices flowing can mean the difference between positive creative focus or stalled, stagnant, and repressed creative potential.

Plane: Mind

Message: Your vision needs to be re-centered on your creative faculties. Step back to see the bigger picture and refocus your efforts on creating that complete image. Nurture your ideas—you are the creator of your world.

15/6 In the positive, the 15/6 is creativity in active motion. True creativity comes from the soul, and the mind is simply a tool to process the soul's creative desire. This is why the five (heart and soul) comes before the mind based creative number (6) in the 15/6.

However, the combination of the six can become particularly volatile and unpredictable if the five (in the weaker or inner position) takes a nose dive into the negative. Instead of heart-centered (5) action (1), the six's drive is based in the moody five, turning the six into pessimistic creativity (gossipy, critical, and judgmental).

Plane: Physical/Soul/Mind

Message: Let your heart be the central guiding force for your creative energy and actions, but be mindful not to let any insecurities take over. The end result may control or restrict your creative juices.

24/6 The certain intuitive power of the two combined with the steady, hardworking four makes the 24/6 doubtless and unstoppable creative energy. In the negative, the two can lean into its traits of doubt, uncertainty, and codependency while the four can become impatience and frustrated. When this happens, the "number of extremes" Six takes a nose dive into the worry wart syndrome, impeding the whole creative process. Keeping the intuitive power of the outer positioned two the central focus is necessary to hold the whole train (2, 4, and 6) on track.

Plane: Soul/Physical/Mind

Message: Allow only your intuition to guide your creative flow. Don't let your mind doubt your intuition; your soul knows precisely what it needs. Confidently take the necessary steps to create what it is whispering to you. You may not be able to see the whole picture now, but know that your soul has the complete image intact and is helping you create it step by step.

33/6 A triple mind plane number combo, the 33/6 is comprised of a double helping of imagination and inspiration (double 3), and the visionary creative master (6). Incredibly inspired creativity that knows no limit is what you get when the 33/6 is in the positive. As the Master Teacher energy, the 33/6 sees the bigger picture (6) and is inspired to create it with gusto (3). In the negative, the self-doubting, self-critical three adds together to form the pessimistic and critical six. This makes the energy a slippery slope into self-sabotaging any creativity. Lacking any physical or soul based energy, many inspired ideas can remain in the realm of the mind (theory) and never brought to fruition. Diligently remaining focused on positively creating will help bring the limitless inspired ideas of the 33/6 to life.

Plane: Mind

Message: There are no limits to your creative power and potential which manifests ideas. Your inspired thinking is contagious. Imagination is the key to your endless creativity.

42/6 Physical effort (4) guided by your inner wisdom (2) will bring your greater vision (6) to life. This is an enduring form of the six, which needs continuous active creative energy to remain in the positive. The "doer" four provides the steady physical momentum for active creative expression. The intuitive two whispers, "You're heading in the right direction. Keep going!" In the negative when the intuitive knowing of the two turns to uncertainty and doubt, the four can become impatient and frustrated, limiting the creative expansion of the six.

Plane: Physical/Soul/Mind

Message: Your greater vision can only be achieved through active participation in life. Even if you can't see precisely where your actions are leading you, never stop moving toward achieving what makes your soul sing. All your hard work will pay off, and your dreams will come true just when you least expect it.

60/6
There is an urgency to refocus on nurturing the self and expressing the creative side. The creative six, combined with the depth of the spiritual zero, reveals a neglect when nurturing creative aspects of your life. Raw creative expression first originates in the soul and is translated by the mind. A balance of both mind and soul is required in the creative process.

Plane: Mind/Soul

Message: Too much focus has been placed on creating for others and not enough on creating what your soul desires. It is time to listen to your soul as it has been omitted from the creative process.

51/6
When it comes to achieving your dreams and the greater image you hold for yourself and your life, you often need to steer off the beaten path based only on a feeling that it's the right way to go. Some of the best life choices are made that way. Whether it is finding your life partner or landing that dream job, most people report synchronicity and chance as the catalyst. This combination of the six is just that: heart-centered risk-taking (5) paired with pioneering action (1) leads to the creation and fulfillment of your wildest dreams (6). If the one also slips into ego-centric mode, the five can become power-seeking or controlling with the outcome being negative energy instead of positive. The heart is never based in ego. Its desire is for the good of all concerned. Focus on following your feelings, (5) and they will always lead you to taking the actions (1) necessary to achieving your life's greater vision (6) and purpose.

Plane: Soul/Physical/Mind

Message: Your heart is urging you to step outside your comfort zone and make a choice your ego doesn't agree with. Take the chance, you won't regret it. It will lead you to something much greater than you are aware of at the present moment.

7 Although seven is all leaping first and thinking later, those leaps aren't as haphazard as they seem. They are driven by the seven's deep, philosophical truth-seeking side. As the base of the Arrow of Spiritual Presence, all action the seven takes is for the purpose of discovering the inherent truth.

Plane: Physical

Message: Take the steps necessary to find the truth you're seeking. It may be the safe road to refrain from action, but it will never lead you to where you desire to be in life.

16/7 The pioneer (1) combined with the visionary (6) adds to form the truth-seeker (7). The word HATE adds to 16/7, and when we tell someone we hate them, it energetically strips them clean of positive energy. There is nothing left to be said; the truth is laid out on the table in plain view. The 16/7 is a profoundly self-reflective energy (7) that seeks truth in a bigger, broader way. This is done through trailblazing ambition (1) and a visionary vantage point (6). It demands nothing less than a truth-filled ah-ha moment. In the negative, the 16/7 creates restlessness, agitation, pessimism, and becomes withdrawn. As the egocentric one and the nit-picky six get fed up, there is little time for reflection, which is required for the seven to reveal deeper truths.

Plane: Physical/Mind

Message: It's time to turn the page in a big way on the things that are not in alignment with your soul. To be truly happy and content you must step into your truth, not someone else's version of it.

25/7

This combination of the seven is chalk full of soulful truth. Joining forces are the two most sensitive and intuitive numbers on the soul plane, which are guiding the seven toward the deeper truth it constantly seeks. Harnessing the power of the intuition (2) then filtering it through the emotions (5) is how we discover the best way to reveal your truth (7).

Plane: Soul/Physical

Message: Your intuition and emotions are wonderful assets when it comes to recognizing truth. Your intuitive and emotional voices are inexplicably tied together, and if it is the truth you seek, one cannot be in disagreement with the other.

34/7

To maintain the search toward truth, we must feel inspired by what we are searching for. This combination of the seven is led by the inspired and imaginative three with a lesser influence of the hardworking four. If the four dips into the negative side, its trait of impatience can put a damper on the inspired light of the three. If this happens, strive to refocus on renewing your sense of inspiration for the journey.

Plane: Mind/Physical

Message: All your efforts will be in vain if you lose sight of what makes your essence come alive. Keep your inspired thoughts front and center as you travel the path to finding your truth.

43/7

Leading through hard work and physical effort is what differentiates this combination from the 34/7, which has inspiration at the helm. Inspired thoughts (3) will keep the fire burning inside us, but the slow and steady progress of the four will ensure we arrive on the doorstep of truth (7).

Plane: Physical/Mental

Message: Your hard work through physical action is slowly building all that you imagined. Maintain your sense of patience as step-by-step progress is the way to unearthing your truth.

52/7

The 52/7 is similar to the 25/7 except it is led more by the heart than the intuition. For this reason, intuition can become clouded by other influences. We can't deny how we feel about something if we're truthful with ourselves. In the negative, the weaker positioned two can overpower and create doubt-filled uncertainty for the emotional and erratic five energy. The search for truth (7) becomes hampered by mixed emotions and a muddled sense of intuition. Realigning with how you feel (5) is the first step to bringing this combination back into alignment. The intuitive self will automatically become clearer when the emotions regain a sense of clarity.

Plane: Soul/Physical

Message: Let your emotions be the translator of the directional messages your soul is whispering to help guide you to your truth.

61/7

This combination represents visionary creativity (6) powered by pioneering ambition (1) for the unified mission of discovering truth (7). The six must constantly create in order to avoid the pull of its strong negative side (number of extremes). Momentum is key to preventing the six from losing sight of the vision, and the one from attempting to go solo, fueled only by blind ambition (without the broad view of the visionary six).

Plane: Mind/Physical

Message: It's important to enjoy the journey through the actions you take to get to where you're going, but don't lose sight of the greater vision of the life you want to create.

70/7 This combination of the seven is the essence of why we are here as seekers of truth (7). We are strengthened by the spiritual power of the symbol of spiritual awareness (0). It is like a neon sign highlighting a need to search for truth in mind, body, and soul.

Plane: Physical/Soul

Message: It is urgent that you find and align with your truth now more than ever. You have put off the search long enough in favor of mundane things that don't serve your higher purpose. It's time to embark on the real journey.

8 As the number of confidence, wisdom, independence, and abundance, eight is the most active soul plane number and has a direct link to the spirit. Tapped into source energy, the pure eight does not doubt, which is a main hindrance in stopping the flow of abundance that is our birthright.

Plane: Soul

Message: Don't doubt the process through which the abundance is flowing to you. If you can't yet see things manifesting, know that it will arrive in the time and fashion that your soul requires.

17/8 The 17/8 is the God frequency, which spells out our overall purpose on earth, regardless of our individual path. As spiritual beings in human form, the essence of why we are here is to verbally express (1) the truths of the divine (7) for the purpose of spreading wisdom and knowledge (8). This develops the soul's growth and evolution.

Plane: Physical/Soul

Message: You are being urged to speak your inner wisdom, sharing it with others. This enables them to recognize their own inner wisdom and understanding.

26/8
This is, by far, the combination of the eight most prone to doubt. Naturally doubtless, when the eight is paired with the intuitive two and the creative six, it forms the "wise sage" energy. Guided by intuition (2) with an eagle's vantage point (6) enables the 26/8 to see the bigger picture. In the negative, the six, in the weaker position, dampens the confidence of the eight with its pessimism and perfectionism. The 26/8 turns into a people-pleasing force that only feels comfortable sharing wisdom if there is no fear of criticism or judgment. Holding the grander vision intact (six has a narrow view in the negative) is critical to keeping the intuition unclouded (2) and the confident eight standing tall it its power as knowledge bearer.

Plane: Soul/Mind

Message: You have important insights to share with the world. Don't concern yourself with whether or not the knowledge will be well received. It is not your place to make sense of the information you are relaying. Just know that your soul only wants you to share it.

35/8
Motivated by pure inspired imagination (3) and the freedom to express (5) its wisdom (8), the 35/8 is a never-ending stream of knowledge and information. In the negative, the 35/8 doubts (3) the power (5) of its wisdom (8).

Plane: Mind/Soul

Message: Don't doubt the powerful inspired messages you're receiving from your soul. Your soul is confident in the messages it is delivering.

44/8

When the assertive and independent eight combines with a double helping of the hardworking four, the 44/8 is ready to take action and deliver knowledge and wisdom. In the negative, the overabundance of the four can become materialistic. This develops an infatuation with purely physical motion, forgetting that the actions are for the greater and deeper purpose of delivering a deeper message.

Plane: Physical/Soul

Message: Action is a pivotal part in sharing your wisdom and knowledge with the world, but take care not to get too wrapped up. This will diminish the purpose, which is to deliver important messages.

53/8

Similar to the 35/8, the 53/8 uses inspired expression to deliver wisdom. However, instead of the imagination (3) leading the process, it is the freedom-seeking number of the heart and emotions (5). Driven by inspired thought and feelings, the 53/8 is less prone to doubt. If the inner number three drops into a negative space, the self-doubt and self-criticism throws the five into the negative qualities of control through power-seeking. Keeping the emotions as the frontrunner guide is important to maintain equilibrium.

Plane: Soul/Mind

Message: You are a compassionate and heart-centered knowledge bearer whose desire is to share what you know. Follow your heart when delivering the messages. If it feels right, it is meant to be shared with that person and at that time.

62/8

The nurturing visionary six is at the head of this energy vibration followed by the sensitive and intuitive two. The combined energies of the six and two greatly soften the confident, assertive, and often detached energy of the strongest soul plane number eight. Expressing through the 62/8 is like a mother gently guiding her child with her knowledge and wisdom. It is not demanding or overbearing, but rather always mindful of whether the information serves the greater good. In the negative, the six can become critical or judgmental and the intuitive power of the two clouds over into uncertainty forcing the eight into assertive aggression. Overbearing motherly energy makes the 62/8 preachy and skewing the purity of the flow of wisdom.

Plane: Mind/Soul

Message: Share the greater vision you are seeing with others, but allow your intuition to guide what you share and with whom. Not everyone is receptive to what you have to share, and the information may cause more harm than good. Use your nurturing instincts to guide you.

71/8 Delivering messages that assist in revealing truth (7) is the first driving force in this combination backed by the fire of the pioneer (1). The determined drive behind the 71/8 makes for one of the most confident combinations of the eight. This energy is not afraid to take risks in the name of sharing important messages from the soul. If the one turns negative, isolating the seven from the eight, distrust and skepticism can make the truth-filled positive into a hesitating and distrustful energy. The seven also shares more through action (guide by example) than by verbal means.

Plane: Physical/Soul

Message: You are full of truth and wisdom. Never hesitate to take action to share of yourself. Others need to hear what you have to say, but, more importantly, be watchful of your actions because they speak louder than your words.

80/8 The eight is the most active of all the soul plane numbers and has a direct link with the soulful energies of the others. Coupled with the power of the symbol of spiritual awareness (0), the 80/8 is a pure and doubtless channel of wisdom. Uninhibited by any other number frequency, the 80/8 is strong and doubtless but also spiritually led (0). This makes it a most divine energy of channeled wisdom directly from the soul.

Plane: Soul

Message: There are important messages of wisdom others in your life need to hear. You have answers that they seek, and it is imperative you share what you know. Let only your soul guide you to share what is necessary in the moment.

9 The single nine is full of ambition, idealism, and responsibility. As the humanitarian number, it only wants to serve to others through its actions. As the highest change number, it represents the idealistic bigger dreamer energy of the mind. In the negative, it can go overboard with putting others before itself. This can often result in necessary changes being put on the backburner. You need to learn to love yourself before you can truly love others, and so the nine must remain attentive to the needs of self in order to stay in the flow of growth and change that it represents.

Plane: Mind

Message: You are being asked to make some changes in your current way of living. One or more parts of your life do not match your inner ideals or dreams. If you are to manifest all that you desire, you need to live in alignment with the energy your soul is sending out.

18/9

The 18/9 is the same frequency as the word love. In unconditional love form, the eight subdues its negative qualities of selfishness and detachment (me, me, me syndrome). This allows the pioneering 1 to take action with the selfless humanitarian nine. The saying "Do anything for love" is appropriate in this case. If the eight flips the negative switch, the selfishness turns the energy of the 18/9 from unconditional to conditional, placing demands and restrictions on the limitless giving of the nine.

Plane: Physical/Soul/Mind

Message: You are being reminded that your actions toward others are meant to be without conditions, restrictions, or limitations. You have your own goals and agenda in life, but ultimately we are all here to be of service to others, not to be concerned with what we receive in return. Through giving we automatically receive.

27/9

The greatest challenge of the 27/9 is to keep the truth-seeking fire burning and not succumb to the negative side of the seven, which is distrust of the self and others. Many great leaders, such as Gandhi and Mother Teresa, have carried the 27/9 energy as their Life Theme Number. Led by the gentle two and guided by the truth-seeking seven, the main essence of the 27/9 is to be of selfless service, helping others discover truth. In the younger years, those who have this main essence energy tend to be followers instead of leaders. They seek outside themselves for the answers until they develop a strong sense of inner self trust through personal experience. With the most active physical number seven in the weaker position, the 27/9 tends to attract personal experience involving hindsight learning (sacrifice, loss and/or hardship).

Plane: Soul/Physical/Mind

Message: All the answers you seek are within you. There is no need to seek in other places or within other people.

36/9 As a triple mind plane energy, the 36/9 has the potential to be the most negative of all the nine combinations. The mind is a powerful tool, but without the intuitive input from the soul plane or the action to bring ideas to life from the physical plane, the mind can run away with itself. In the positive, the imaginative three joins hands with the visionary six to form the selfless humanitarian number nine. In the negative, it can become self-doubting (3), pessimistic (6) and judgmental (9), making it not capable of serving others. Often those who carry the 36/9 as their main essence need to be surrounded by positive people, places, and things in order to stay in the positive.

Plane: Mind

Message: Surround yourself only with positive things, as it will serve as the inspirational catalyst in making life changes.

45/9 The nine determined, idealistic, and justice-seeking, wanting to right the wrongs of the world. All actions (4) need to be heart-centered (5) in order to truly be of selfless service to others (9). In the negative, the materialistic four and the power-seeking five can turn the nine into an opinionated, bossy tyrant. Equilibrium of the emotions is the positive anchor of the 45/9 and will keep it moving smoothly along.

Plane: Physical/Soul/Mind

Message: Let your emotions guide your actions in choosing what is right and wrong.

54/9 Impatient with the effort it takes to make long term changes is caused by the four being in the weaker position. Even more so than the 45/9, the 54/9 can succumb to dominating behaviors (5) and impatient frustration (4), refocusing the nine on the trait of black and white thinking (idealism).

Plane: Soul/Physical/Mind

Message: Do what you feel is the right choice in the moment, but know that the easy route isn't always the best one. Much satisfaction can be gained from putting in time and effort into realizing your dreams.

63/9 Similar to the 36/9, the 63/9 can become way too mindfully top heavy because it is solely comprised of mind energy. The advantage of the 63/9 is that the front row energy is the visionary six, which can see the greater scheme of things. Guided by the broader overall vision (6) and inspired thinking (3), compliments the nine best, as it is the big dreamer. Three can be overly enthusiastic, and the nine isn't the most practical. This makes the six the great balancer in this number combination. Much like the 36/9, while in the negative the 63/9 can become pessimistic (6), doubtful (3), and lose sight of the bigger picture. If the six is not actively creating it easily loses its way, so this is the energy of focus in both combinations.

Plane: Mind

Message: Base your change-filled actions on the greater vision of what you want to achieve for yourself and others. Allow that image to be the main inspiration behind all that you do.

72/9 Unlike the 27/9, which often has issues with trust, the 72/9 starts off with a firm footing of trust with the seven in the outer position. The seven is followed by the number of intuition to strengthen the sense of trust. Instead of the uncertainty, it manifests as a disconnection from the intuitive self. In the positive, this very active number combination, with the most active physical plane number seven leading the pack, quietly encouraged by the supportive two and inspired by the base number nine, it is a well oiled machine. In order to achieve what we desire, we need to think it, feel it, and do it—and this combo has all three required forces.

Plane: Physical/Soul/Mind

Message: You are an unstoppable force driven by your soul's desires. Dream big and keep going. Your thoughts, feelings, and actions are in perfect sync with each other.

81/9 While in the negative, this is potentially the most arrogant of all the nine combinations. The confident, assertive, and doubtless eight is followed by the isolating, pioneering, and often egocentric one. This forms the opinionated and narrow-minded nine. In the positive, the doubtless purity of the number of wisdom (8) as guide, driven by the active ambition of the (1) creates the perfect atmosphere for the nine. In this combination, the one is the glue holding everything together. As long as the actions taken don't become focused only on personal achievement, the 81/9 remains the wisest and most profound of all nine energies.

Plane: Soul/Physical/Mind

Message: Act only on the wise messages from your soul, which are constantly guiding you. This will assist you in bringing your grand life plan to fruition. Differentiating between whether the message is from the heart or the head is easy; ask your soul what it wants, and it will answer without hesitation or doubt.

90/9 One of the most common derailments of the progress of the big dreaming nine is a lack of connection to the soul for guidance. The idealistic nine tends to think it has all the answers. The joining together of the most active mind number (9) with the symbol of spiritual awareness (0) can be highlighting a need for more spiritual involvement in the nine's actions. It can also provide much needed balance from an energetic perspective. The soul doesn't suffer from regret, but the nine certainly does. With blind determination (head of Arrow of Determined Effort) and fiercely opinionated thinking, the nine can be off on a tangent if the soul isn't consulted. When in the positive and both the nine and zero are working in harmony, the nine becomes the genius and the inventor. This brings workable ideas to life that have never been dreamt before.

Plane: Mind/Soul

Message: The power of the mind is a great gift, but always remember that your soul is the ultimate creator. The mind is merely a tool through which the soul works. Allowing the mind to be the ruling force in your life will lead you off track.

CONCLUSION

Writer and poet Ralph Waldo Emerson, who was a creative visionary six essence, said "Life is a journey, not a destination." This book is a tool to help you navigate the journey by showing you who you truly are and what you're here on Earth to accomplish. What you choose to do with that information is up to you.

The best part about life is the option of choice. There are endless paths to take, and we all have a choice in regards to everything we think, say, and do. The choices we make moment by moment shape our life experiences, which in turn shapes our destiny. We are in total control of *how* our life unfolds, but the more knowledge we have, the more precise our sights can be set on all that we desire.

I believe there are no coincidences, and that everything happens for a reason in divine timing. Over a decade ago I began dreaming in numbers, as it was time for me to embrace my purpose. As a pure 30/3 essence, I am the inspirationalist. I am happiest when I can uplift and inspire others, showing them how beautiful and talented they are. I have been told by many that I light up when I talk about the numbers. I know without a doubt that sharing the knowledge contained in the numbers is my calling.

I am honored to be the one to reveal your soul numbers and help you decipher the messages from your inner self to successful navigate life. Enjoy the journey.

ACKNOWLEDGMENTS

I'd like to give my sincerest, grandest thank-you to the following souls who played a big part in the birth of this book:

Carrie White, my 11:11 sister; Elizabeth Isaacs for a doing such a superb editing job on extremely short notice; my literary manager, Italia Gandolfo for being amazing at everything; Marie D. Jones, my inspiration to keep going for my dreams with gusto; Treva Etienne, my Earth Guide friend who taught me how important it is to live my truth; Catherine Scott for giving me my start in the world of celebrity; Michelle Russell, my Earth Angel and the most talented psychic medium in the universe who helped me plant the seed of all that I have achieved. Hats off to my husband Will for his immense patience and being my rock who never doubted even my craziest dreams. Love to my children for choosing me to be their guardian and being exactly who they came into this world to be, making me a better parent and person in the process. Lastly, much love and light to the Angels who have been ever-present by my side throughout life's journey.

GLOSSARY OF TERMS

Energy – The capacity of a physical system to do work; power.

Ego – The division of the psyche that is conscious, most immediately controls thought and behavior and is most in touch with external reality.

Spirit – The vital principle or animating force within living beings (another word for the soul).

Vibration - A rapid linear motion of a particle or of an elastic solid about an equilibrium position.

Manifest – to make clear, noticeable, distinguishable to the senses, bring to awareness.

Numerology – The Science of Numbers as originally developed by Greek Mathematician and Philosopher Pythagoras who believed all things are numbers at their base; a system utilizing numbers to represent energy patterns in all things.

Frequency – The number of times a vibration repeats itself in a specified time dictates its frequency. For example, we tune in our radio to the particular radio frequency the station is broadcasting. Frequencies are often measured in hertz.

Destiny – A decided or predetermined path; fate.

Reality – The quality or state of being real or true.

Metaphysical - the transcendent or referring to something beyond what the traditional five senses can perceive.

Essence – the basis, core or true fundamental nature of something.

RECOMMENDED READING

Angel Numbers 101: The Meaning of 111, 123, 444, and Other Number Sequences (Doreen Virtue, Hay House, Jun 12, 2008)

11:11 the Time Prompt Phenomenon: The Meaning Behind Mysterious Signs, Sequences, and Synchronicities (Marie D. Jones/ Larry Flaxman, New Page Books, February 1, 2009)

The Life You Were Born to Live: A Guide to Finding Your Life Purpose (Dan Millman, HJ Kramer, Feb 8 1995)

Law of Attraction: The Science of Attracting More of What You Want and Less of What You Don't (Michael J. Losier, Grand Central Life & Style, May 12 2010)

BIBLIOGRAPHY

[1] "Wholeness and the Implicate Order," David Bohm, November 17, 2002, Routledge

[2] http://plato.stanford.edu/entries/pythagoras/

[3] Marshak, A., *The Roots of Civilisation; Cognitive Beginnings of Man's First Art, Symbol and Notation*, (Weidenfeld & Nicolson, London: 1972), 81ff.

[4] http://www.anciv.info/mesopotamia/science-and-technology-in-mesopotamia.html

[5] http://www.factualworld.com/article/Buddhist_prayer_beads

[6] All objects in our universe are composed of vibrating filaments (strings) and membranes (branes) of energy. http://www.dummies.com/how-to/content/string-theory-for-dummies-cheat-sheet.html

[7] http://www.newyorker.com/archive/2002/08/19/020819craw_artworld

[8] http://www.psychologytoday.com/blog/everyday-mind-reading/200901/where-is-womens-intuition

[9] http://www.teachingenglish.org.uk/articles/non-verbal-communication

[10] http://www.2012-spiritual-growth-prophecies.com/numerology-meanings-2.html#Numerology-Meaning-Pythagoras

[11] http://reluctant-messenger.com/reincarnation-proof.htm#interview

ABOUT THE AUTHOR

Michelle Arbeau is an internationally known celebrity numerologist, inspirational speaker, and radio and TV host. She has a clientele base that stretches around the globe, with clients ranging from those seeking purpose and direction to successful professionals and celebrities wanting to fine-tune their careers and personal lives. Some of her celebrity clientele include *Twilight* vampires Judi Shekoni and Amadou Ly, *Big Bang Theory* actress Alice Amter, NBC director Ricky Powell, *Pirates of the Caribbean* actor Treva Etienne, *A League of their Own* actress Lori Petty, and celebrity stylist Carrie White. A media favorite who is considered an expert in her field, she is frequently a guest on national media outlets such as CBC Radio, CTV *Morning Live*, and *Breakfast Television*. She has spoken on a wide range of topics from Friday the 13th to predicting Obama's re-election.

Arbeau's love of numbers and numerology happened in a very synchronistic way. After a near-death experience at the age of four, she began to experience psychic phenomena that continued throughout her early life. Lacking guidance and support, she pushed her premonitions and intuitive information aside until her early twenties, when she suddenly began dreaming in numbers every single night. Knowing these were messages from the spiritual realm, she sought out their meaning on the Internet. Stumbling upon numerology, she discovered that the messages were direct answers to her life issues. Amazed by the accuracy of the numerical messages, Arbeau began a love affair with the world of numbers. She now teaches Power of Numbers workshops in venues throughout North America, from New York City to Los Angeles, and also shares her knowledge of numbers in private client sessions.

OPEN ROAD
INTEGRATED MEDIA

Open Road Integrated Media is a digital publisher and multimedia content company. Open Road creates connections between authors and their audiences by marketing its ebooks through a new proprietary online platform, which uses premium video content and social media.

CPSIA information can be obtained
at www.ICGtesting.com
Printed in the USA
JSHW040330171221
21299JS00003B/254

9 781497 660984